D0435185

With All Deliberate Speed:
Court-ordered Busing and American Schools

4967 6298 9/12

CIVIL RIGHTS MOVEMENT

With All Deliberate Speed: Court-ordered Busing and American Schools

David Aretha

MORGAN REYNOLDS
PUBLISHING

Greensboro, North Carolina

Students in lines at the Grew Elementary School in Boston on September 10, 1965. The African American students were placed in the lines by adults after they were refused entrance to the school by Principal Martin Feeney. The door was closed and all the youngsters, both white and black, were left outside.

CIVIL RIGHTS MOVEMENT
With All Deliberate Speed:
Court-ordered Busing and American Schools

Copyright © 2012 by Morgan Reynolds Publishing

Library of Congress Cataloging-in-Publication Data

Aretha, David.
With all deliberate speed : court-ordered busing and American schools /
by David Aretha.
     p. cm.
Includes bibliographical references and index.
ISBN 978-1-59935-181-0 -- ISBN 978-1-59935-217-6 (e-book)
1. Busing for school integration--United States--History--Juvenile
literature. 2. School integration--United States--History--Juvenile
literature. I. Title.
LC214.5.A74 2012
379.2'630973--dc23

                                        2011019530

PRINTED IN THE UNITED STATES OF AMERICA
First Edition

Book cover and interior designed by:
Ed Morgan, navyblue design studio
Greensboro, NC

Table of Contents

About five hundred men took part in a "Men's March Against Forced Busing" in the Charlestown section of Boston, in May 1976.

chapter 1

The "Master Plan"

On the morning of April 5, 1976, some two hundred white students headed to downtown Boston. They gathered at city hall for yet another protest against court-mandated busing, a practice that had divided the city for two years. White students had been bused to schools in inner-city black neighborhoods, and black students were sent to schools in the poor white areas. Seemingly everybody involved hated the court-mandated busing fiasco, especially the white families.

On April 5, the students and accompanying adults brought a list of demands to city hall. One student, who lived in a white working-class section of the city called South Boston, brought a large American flag on a long pole. The whites of South Boston felt especially patriotic during this crisis. According to their way of thinking, a judge, in the name of equal rights for African Americans, had infringed on *their* rights. White Bostonians sang "God Bless America" during their protests and waved the Stars and Stripes.

Whites affected by busing cursed the name of W. Arthur Garrity Jr., the U.S. District Court judge who had issued his "Master Plan" in Boston on June 21, 1974. But Garrity was well protected by federal marshals at his home in the wealthy suburb of Wellesley. Black Americans had no such protection. They often fell victim to the whites' wrath, and they sometimes engaged in reciprocal violence.

As the protesters filed out of city hall, they came across a group of black students. "Epithets flew," wrote author Louis P. Masur, "as did pieces of food—donuts, cookies, apples." Amid the conflict, Ted Landsmark, a black attorney in a three-piece suit, entered the scene. Immediately, the whites went after Landsmark, perhaps because they saw him as a symbol of the civil rights leadership that had pushed for desegregation plans.

As two white protesters yelled "get the nigger," the students grabbed, kicked, and punched Landsmark, smashing his glasses and breaking his nose. During the assault, the student with the flag waved it in front of Landsmark, a moment frozen in time by photographer Stanley Forman of the *Boston Herald American*. In Forman's photograph, it looks like the student—with his long hair flowing backward—is about to thrust the flagpole like a spear into the gut of the black attorney, whose arms are secured behind his back by a protester.

The next day, the photograph was splashed across the front pages of the *Herald American*, *Washington Post*, *Chicago Tribune*, and other newspapers. *Oh, my God* was undoubtedly the response. What was America coming to? In 1976, as the nation celebrated the Bicentennial—in the city of Paul Revere and the Battle of Bunker Hill—a white man was seemingly attacking a black man with the American flag. It was as if the civil rights movement had never happened.

The nation had seen advancements in school equality since 1954, when the U.S. Supreme Court ruled on *Brown v. Board of Education*. Prior to that ruling, public schools in the South and some other cities across the nation were segregated. White students would go to one school and black children learned in a different school. With the *Brown* decision, the Supreme Court sent shockwaves through the South when it announced that segregated public schools were unconstitutional.

A 1955 photograph showing the integrated
Barnard School in Washington, D.C.

Eventually, southern school systems began to integrate in the 1950s and '60s. In many communities, black students were bused to predominantly white schools in order to achieve integration. Southern school boards and parents who resisted were deemed "racist" by the rest of the nation. But in the 1970s, when federal courts started to order southern and northern districts to desegregate their schools, the nation was in an uproar.

In Boston, the horrors started on September 12, 1974, the first day of court-ordered busing. In the South Boston neighborhood, whites greeted incoming black students by throwing rocks at their buses' windows, injuring nine. Ellen Jackson, who headed a community center in the Boston neighborhood of Roxbury, recalled when black elementary students returned there after their first day in a white school:

> When the kids came, everybody just broke out in tears and started crying. The kids were crying. They had glass in their hair. They were scared. And they were shivering and crying. Talking about they wanted to go home. We tried to gently usher them into the auditorium. And wipe off the little bit of bruises that they had. Small bruises and the dirt. Picked the glass out of their hair.

At several Boston high schools, racial strife got so bad that fights broke out on a daily basis. At South Boston High School, upwards of three hundred police officers patrolled the grounds. At some high schools, metal detectors were installed, and snipers took positions on rooftops. "Every day when I get up," said one teacher, "it's like getting up to go to prison."

In the second half of the twentieth century, hundreds of desegregation plans were implemented across the country, many of them involving busing. Sociologist David J. Armor called busing "the most unpopular, least successful . . . national policy since Prohibition." Most people despised the practice.

A 1981 CBS/*New York Times* poll found that 77 percent of Americans opposed busing as a way to achieve integration and only 17 percent favored it. Most African Americans were against busing, even though it was meant to help black students.

As the Boston crisis dragged on, pundits continuously debated the merits of busing. Opined social scientist Robert L. Crain in 1980, "I've looked at almost 100 analyses of student achievement as a result of desegregation, and the overall conclusion of the vast majority is that blacks are helped and whites are not hurt."

"That's simply not true," responded Representative-elect Bobbi Fiedler of Los Angeles. "What you get is tremendous turmoil, lots of disciplinary problems, and a bad academic atmosphere."

Many critics of school busing believe that too much emphasis has been put on race in the classroom—that black students just need good schools; they don't need to sit next to white kids to get a good education. Opponents lament all the money spent on transportation, and how students waste up to an hour or two a day on the bus. That busing shatters black communities, as the kids don't share the local school with their neighborhood friends. Busing means that parents have a much harder time being involved with the school since it is often far away and leads not to harmonious diversity but to tensions between blacks and whites. Moreover, it has put children in dangerous situations. The psychological and emotional damage to white and especially black children, who have been made to feel unwanted and inferior, has been enormous. Such trauma, the critics say, can alienate students from learning and society and lead to a greater dropout rate.

The list of complaints goes on and on. In many cities, busing exacerbated "white flight," meaning white families fled to the suburbs in order to avoid busing or the desegregation

A 1975 photograph of a police officer standing guard while African American students of South Boston High School climb into the buses, drawn right up to the school doors, that will take them home after classes

of their schools. White flight causes multiple problems. For one, it creates an even more segregated community. Moreover, when wealthier white families leave, the city has less tax revenue. In such places as Detroit and Cleveland, the white flight of the 1960s to 1980s resulted in impoverished, rundown cities.

Busing still has had its supporters. Proponents claim that segregated schools have always been harmful to African American students. With relatively few exceptions, black schools have been poorly funded and often dilapidated. They have attracted inferior teachers, and the supplies and opportunities have been subpar. Psychologists have suggested that being relegated to a segregated school and unwelcome in white schools, is psychologically damaging to black students.

With busing, proponents say, inner-city black students have the chance to reap the benefits of a higher social status. They can broaden their horizons and learn how to mix socially with whites, which would benefit them in the working world. They are also on a better path to college and a fruitful career.

Busing is an often-misunderstood phenomenon. It didn't just happen in Boston in the 1970s; desegregation efforts have been implemented by more than one thousand American school systems since 1954. Busing hasn't always been mandated by federal courts; school systems have voluntarily implemented busing plans in about half the cases. Not all busing plans have been the same, and not every busing effort has been considered a failure. The massive busing program in Charlotte, North Carolina, for example, was deemed a major success.

The story of busing is endlessly fascinating. The more you explore, the more you learn about race relations, civil rights, education, politics, and what has been in the hearts and minds of everyday Americans. It's also important to understand that there was a reason for all the busing madness, and its name was Jim Crow.

chapter 2

How Busing Began

Back in the 1930s, the more fortunate black schoolchildren learned in all-black public schools. Others learned, or at least tried to, wherever adults could find space, such as churches or abandoned stores. Wrote Catherine Reef in *Education and Learning in America*, all the schools for African Americans in Mississippi and elsewhere "lacked furniture and such basic equipment as books, blackboards, and maps. Four empty walls, crude benches, an old wood-burning stove, and painted boards serving as a chalkboard were the norm in African-American schools."

African American Rossie T. Hollis knew this injustice firsthand. She recalled "how we walked miles on the cold mornings to a school with one small stove which often smoked until water ran out of our eyes."

While the all-white schools in the South, and many other areas in the United States, were often underfunded and substandard, the all-black schools were almost always inferior. Black children suffered the injustice of substandard education for two reasons: State and local governments deliberately short-changed funding for black schools, and—at least until the 1950s—the federal government allowed the injustice to continue.

After the Civil War, the U.S. Congress passed three amendments on behalf of African Americans. The Thirteenth Amendment prohibited slavery, the Fourteenth granted citizenship to African Americans, and the Fifteenth allowed black men to vote. Most southern whites could not handle these abrupt changes. Blacks had been enslaved in the South from the 1600s, and whites had grown accustomed to the southern caste system. To grant blacks full citizenship meant that they could not be used as free laborers. The black population in certain parts of the South was so large that whites worried that black men would be elected to office and thus be "in charge."

Moreover, many whites obsessed over the thought of black men having sexual relations with white women. Said Arkansas Governor Jeff Davis in 1904, "I want to say that I would rather tear, screaming from her mother's arms, my little daughter and bury her alive than to see her arm and arm with the best nigger on earth."

Legislatures in former Confederate states passed laws to create "Black Codes," which assured that blacks could not rent land, bear arms, or

Governor Jeff Davis

serve on juries. Through sharecropping, whites hired blacks to work on their land for pitiful wages. They charged the black workers so much for equipment, food, and other items that the workers were perpetually indebted to them. Blacks who tried to vote would face economic or physical consequences. Those who risked relations with a white woman could be beaten or lynched.

In the 1880s, southern states began to pass segregation laws. These laws officially confined black citizens to separate public facilities, such as railway coaches, restaurants, theaters, outhouses, and schools. State legislatures claimed that the laws met the mandate of the Fourteenth Amendment, which says, "No State shall make or enforce any law which shall abridge the privileges or immunities of citizens of the United States; nor shall any State deprive any person of life, liberty, or property, without due process of law. . . ." They met that requirement, the states' attorneys said, because while the facilities for blacks were separate, they were of equal quality.

In the 1896 segregation suit *Plessy v. Ferguson*, the U.S. Supreme Court ruled that "separate but equal" facilities were indeed acceptable. Up through the mid-1900s, a "Jim Crow" (segregated) caste system flourished in the South and other parts of the country. But while black facilities—including schools—were separate, they were hardly ever equal.

Southern governments spent much more money on white schools than on black schools. In 1940, the eight Deep South states spent more than twice as much money on each white student than on each black pupil. In fact, four of the eight states spent at least three times as much. In Mississippi, the state spent $513 per white student and a mere $89 for each black student—a six-to-one ratio.

Outside of the South, segregation was not as blatant but it certainly existed. Prior to 1951, Arizona required segregated schools. Kansas and New Mexico permitted segregated schools. Wyoming permitted them if the local black population was large. Indiana gave its school boards the choice of segregation. Even though Illinois prohibited segregated schools, many counties allowed the practice anyway.

In discussing the topic, historians talk about *de jure* segregation and *de facto* segregation. De jure means "by law." In the South, segregation was on the books. De facto means "by custom." Outside the South, de facto segregation was commonplace, resulting in schools that were all or nearly all white and other schools that were 100 percent black or close to it.

Many districts engaged in gerrymandering, the practice of drawing district lines unfairly to suit one's advantage. In addition, housing segregation resulted in school segregation. Legally until 1948, and subtly afterward, real estate agents and homeowners often refused to allow African Americans to buy in certain suburbs or city neighborhoods. Realizing that they weren't welcomed in the "nice" areas, they settled in black neighborhoods, where the schools were usually inferior. Cities typically built public housing, which would be dominated by minority residents, in the "less desirable" parts of the city.

Charles T. Clotfelter, author of *After Brown: The Rise and Retreat of School Desegregation*, wrote about "the judicious placement of newly constructed schools." A city might build one school in the heart of a white neighborhood and another in the middle of a black community (as opposed to building one school in the middle), which would reinforce segregation. In the big cities of the East and Midwest, millions of white students attended Catholic schools, which further upset the racial balance of public schools.

A black girl and a white girl study a sign in the integrated Long Island community of Lakeview, New York, in April 1962. It reads "Negroes! This community could become another ghetto. You owe it to your 'family' to buy in another community." The sign was an attempt to keep blacks from exceeding the number of whites who wanted to live in an integrated town.

As in the South, northern blacks were not just separated; they usually received an inferior education. In 1955, the New York Public Education Association compared the city's predominantly white (less than 10 percent black and Puerto Rican) and predominantly minority (90 percent or more black and Puerto Rican) public schools. Compared to the white schools, the minority schools were, on average, twelve years older (forty-three to thirty-one years) and much more crowded (forty-six square feet per pupil to 103 square feet). The white schools had more tenured teachers (78 to 50 percent) and relied on fewer substitute teachers (8 to 18 percent).

A 1917 photograph of seventy-five sixth grade black children crowded into one small room in an old store building with one teacher in Muskogee, Oklahoma

Not only were the funding and quality of education grossly unequal in both the North and the South, but the "separate" aspect had a debilitating effect. This was famously illustrated in the 1940s "doll tests" of psychologists Kenneth and Mamie Clark. Over and over, the Clarks found that black children preferred playing with white dolls instead of black dolls. They tended to define the white dolls as pretty and the black dolls as ugly. Scholars concluded that segregation, in which blacks were removed from white society and treated as inferior, damaged African Americans psychologically.

The dismantling of school segregation did not begin with that 1954 *Brown* case. It started years earlier through the determined efforts of the National Association for the Advancement of Colored People (NAACP). From 1926 to 1928, the NAACP journal *The Crisis* published a series of articles that revealed the great disparity in school financing in several southern states. *Crisis* editor W. E .B. Du Bois urged the NAACP to initiate a movement to "secure justice" for black schoolchildren. Two black NAACP attorneys, Charles Houston and Thurgood Marshall, would answer the call, resulting in cases that would rise to the U.S. Supreme Court.

In 1938, Houston prevailed in the Supreme Court case *Missouri ex rel Gaines v. Canada*. The court agreed that the state of Missouri had to provide law school access to qualified black applicant Lloyd L. Gaines. The state capitulated. But instead of admitting Gaines to the law school of his choice, at the University of Missouri, the state created a law school just for him at all-black Lincoln University.

Tireless attorney Marshall believed that "[e]qual means getting the same thing, at the same time, and in the same place." In 1950, Marshall won two Supreme Court cases, *McLaurin v. Oklahoma State Regents* and *Sweatt v. Painter*. The court ruled that the University of Oklahoma could not segregate

G. W. McLaurin in his graduate school classroom (he had been forced to sit in the "Negro row"). In *Sweatt*, the court decided that the state's hastily created black law school did not give African Americans "equal" education to whites. The court forced the University of Texas Law School to admit plaintiff Herman Marion Sweatt.

Marshall chiseled away at the stone wall of school segregation. In *Brown v. Board of Education*, he brought out the dynamite.

The *Brown* case was actually a conglomerate of four segregation cases that the Supreme Court reviewed at once. *Brown* referred to Reverend Oliver Brown, a black resident of Topeka, Kansas. His young daughters, Linda and Terry, could not attend the public white school in their neighborhood. Instead, they had to take a long, dangerous walk through a railroad switchyard in order to catch a bus that would drive them to an all-black public school. Years later, busing proponents would point out the irony: Americans as a whole hadn't much cared when black kids were bused to black schools, but they were aghast when busing affected white students.

During the *Brown* proceedings, Marshall discussed the Clarks' doll study, which seemed to indicate that segregation had negative psychological effects on African Americans. His argument was persuasive. Earl Warren, a recently appointed chief justice, announced the court's ruling. "We conclude, unanimously, that in the field of public education the doctrine of 'separate but equal' has no place," he said. "Separate educational facilities are inherently unequal."

In what many would hail as the most important Supreme Court decision of the twentieth century, the Warren Court had ruled that segregated public schools were unconstitutional. The court remanded the matter to district courts, which should, Warren said, "enter such orders and decrees consistent with this opinion as are necessary and proper to admit [students] to public schools on a racially nondiscriminatory basis with all deliberate speed."

The words *all deliberate speed* would become the bane of integrationists, because many southern lawmakers planned to take years to integrate their schools. Some cities, such as Washington and Baltimore, obeyed the ruling immediately. But the mood throughout most of the South was one of defiance. Whites in Dixie referred to the day of the Supreme Court's ruling as "Black Monday." Declared an editorial in the *Jackson* (Mississippi) *Daily News*, "Human blood may stain southern soil in many places because of this decision, but the dark red stains of that blood will be on the marble of the United States Supreme Court Building."

Why were Southerners so resistant? According to President Dwight Eisenhower, in an aside to Justice Earl Warren, southern whites wanted to make sure that "their sweet little white girls are not required to sit in school alongside some big black buck." Many whites might not have expressed it so crudely, but school segregationists frequently railed against "race mixing" and the "inevitable" results: black males having sex with white females, an act that in the past had led to hundreds of lynchings, and impregnating them, which they said would lead to the unthinkable "mongrelization" of the human race.

Today, most of us view such thinking as barbaric and disgusting. But history has shown that when a racial caste system has been in place for hundreds of years, the privileged race will typically view the suppressed race as inherently inferior.

Feeling that their way of life was under attack, whites in 1954 created the White Citizens' Council (WCC), with branches across the South. Considered more reputable than the Ku Klux Klan but derided by critics as the "white-collar Klan," the WCC flexed its political and economic power. They fought against segregation and made sure that desegregation activists lost their jobs. Violence against black Americans

26

An angry mob tries to overturn a car carrying blacks in Clinton, Tennessee, in August 1956. The driver sped away before the doors were opened. The mob was motivated by the White Citizens' Council leader who spoke against integration at Clinton High School.

also intensified after the *Brown* ruling, as exemplified by the murder of fourteen-year-old African American Emmett Till in Mississippi in 1955.

On May 31, 1955, the U.S. Supreme Court, in *Brown II*, established guidelines for undoing segregated public education, although it did not establish a timetable. In March 1956, nineteen U.S. senators and eighty-one U.S. representatives signed the Southern Manifesto, which sought to repeal the Supreme Court's decisions on school segregation. Their efforts would not succeed, but southern states in the Deep South continued to resist.

Schools became battlegrounds, most notably in Little Rock, Arkansas, in 1957. President Eisenhower had to call in the national guard to help nine African American students integrate Central High School. "They've gone in," a white woman cried on that fateful day in September 1957. "Oh, God, the niggers are in the school."

Many cities desegregated their schools peacefully, particularly those in the north-south border states. But in the Deep South, they continued to put up a fight. Many school districts tried to circumvent the law by creating "freedom of choice" plans. Black students could transfer to other schools in their district if certain criteria were met (which was rare). By 1960, only 0.2 percent of the South's black students were actually going to schools with whites.

Resistance was so intense in Clinton, Tennessee, that segregationists bombed the public high school. Some southern communities built private schools for their white students. In Prince Edward County, Virginia, officials decided to shut down the public school system as an alternative to integrating it. They built a private academy for white students, while most black students went without an education (a small percentage learned in makeshift schools established by the NAACP and black ministers). Prince Edward's public schools were closed from 1959 to 1964.

In South Carolina and Alabama, schools weren't desegregated until September 1963. Alabama governor George Wallace finally capitulated when President John F. Kennedy federalized the Alabama National Guard. But even then, the results were limited. By 1964, only 1.2 percent of Alabama's black students were attending schools with whites.

Rarely discussed in history books is the NAACP's attempt to desegregate *non*-southern school systems during this era. In 1961-62, that organization took action to challenge segregated schools in fifty-five school districts in the Midwest, West, and Northeast. The NAACP didn't care if it was *de jure* or *de facto*. Segregation was segregation, and they wanted it to end.

By 1964, the power of the civil rights movement—led by Martin Luther King Jr. and carried out by thousands of justice-seeking activists—had turned the country against segregation. On July 2, President Lyndon Johnson signed the Civil Rights Act of 1964. The legislation not only spelled doom for the Jim Crow caste system, but it signaled the beginning of massive school desegregation—not just in the South but across the United States.

A policeman flanks three
African American high
school seniors as they arrive
for classes at the previously
all-white Bogalusa High
School in Bogalusa,
Louisiana, in
September 1965.

chapter 3

Rev Up the Buses

For civil rights activists, the road to the Civil Rights Act of 1964 was a long haul. They endured beatings during their sit-ins and Freedom Rides, and thousands were arrested during hundreds of protests. Workers in Birmingham, Alabama, blasted young protesters with fire hoses, and a quarter-million justice seekers trekked to Washington to hear Martin Luther King's "I Have a Dream" speech. All these efforts, as well as the general public's support of them, inspired Congress to pass the historic legislation.

The Civil Rights Act was most famous for outlawing discrimination in public facilities. As a result of the act, and the Voting Rights Act of 1965, segregation in the South gradually diminished.

The Civil Rights Act also included language about education. It authorized the Department of Health, Education, and Welfare to withhold funds to any district that excluded students from schools on the basis of race. It also authorized the attorney general to initiate class-action lawsuits against schools that did not conform to the law.

The Civil Rights March in Washington, D.C., in 1963

The Civil Rights Act showed that after ten years, the federal government was finally getting serious about dismantling segregated schools. But that was only the beginning. In 1965, Congress passed the Elementary and Secondary Education Act. According to this legislation, schools with around 40 percent of low-income students were qualified to receive federal funding. This provided an incentive to school districts to accept more black students, the majority of whom were low-income.

The 1966 "Coleman Report" had a powerful influence on the federal government's education policy. The U.S. Department of Education had commissioned renowned sociologist James Coleman and other scholars to create a report on educational equality in the United States. After studying data on several hundred thousand students, they released the report "Equality of Educational Opportunity," aka the Coleman Report.

The report found that the *amount* of school funding had little effect on students' achievement. Parochial school officials likely were not surprised, since their students often outperformed public school kids even though their schools operated on shoestring budgets. The Coleman Report also found that funding for predominantly black schools had become almost the same as funding for white schools. Over the years, it was believed, southern school districts had upped the funding of black schools to fend off the pro-integrationists.

So why were the test scores of African American students still lower than whites? The Coleman Report said that test scores correlated with the children's family background and socioeconomic status, and that black students in racially mixed classrooms performed better than those in all-black and typically poorer schools. In fact, the report asserted that the number-one indicator of a minority or lower-class student's success was the educational level of his or her classmates. In theory, then, if black kids from impoverished inner cities were bused to largely white schools, they would get better test scores.

The report was hugely influential. Said Karl Alexander, a Johns Hopkins University sociology professor and a colleague of the report's author, "Coleman, more than anyone else, was at the forefront of directing the importance of the social context of education."

With Coleman's data to work from, anti-segregationists pushed forward in the courts. The U.S. Supreme Court forced the action in *Green v. School Board of New Kent County* (1968). Calvin Green, the plaintiff in the case, contended that the freedom-of-choice plan in his county made desegregation a sham. The county had two high schools, and the housing patterns were not segregated. Yet due to the freedom-of-choice plan, one high school was mostly white, and the other was all black.

Clearly, the court found, the county was sidestepping its constitutional duty to desegregate—just like many other school systems had done. Warren's court would have none of it. The court found that "the state, acting through the local school and school officials, organized and operated a dual system, part 'white' and part 'Negro'" in "every facet of school operations—faculty, staff, transportation, extracurricular activities and facilities."

The freedom-of-choice plan was not enough, the court asserted. It stressed the need for an "affirmative duty to take whatever steps might be necessary to convert to a unitary system in which racial discrimination would be eliminated root and branch." Fourteen years after *Brown*, the court demanded desegregation as soon as possible. Associate Justice William Brennan wrote, "The burden on a school board today is to come forward with a plan that promises realistically to work, and promises realistically to work now." Brennan later wrote privately, "When this opinion is handed down, the traffic light will have changed from *Brown* to *Green*. Amen!"

The Supreme Court again showed its eagerness to end segregated schooling with *Alexander v. Holmes County Board of Education* (1969). Thirty-three Mississippi school districts wanted to postpone desegregation plans to September 1970, but the high court said no. The Supreme Court insisted that "each of the school districts here involved may no longer operate a dual school system based on race or color." The court directed that the school systems "begin immediately to operate as unitary school systems within which no person is to be effectively excluded from any school because of race or color." The key word in *Alexander v. Holmes* was immediately.

Together, the Civil Rights Act, Elementary and Secondary Education Act, and federal court cases had a strong effect on getting schools to desegregate, particularly in the South. From 1968 to 1972, the number of black students attending minority schools (90 percent or more minority) in the South dropped from 78 percent to 25 percent. To achieve integration, thousands of students were assigned to different schools. In many cases, they were bused to reach their destinations.

From Nashville to Little Rock, from Tampa to Oklahoma City, school districts desegregated en masse in the late 1960s and early 1970s. One of the most interesting cases occurred in Charlotte, North Carolina. For one reason, it led to an important Supreme Court case. In addition, it was one of the rare cities where busing was deemed a success.

Charlotte, North Carolina

The Charlotte-Mecklenburg school district included not just the central city but also Mecklenburg County. The white-black ratio of students was roughly 70-30, with 14,000 students attending schools that were 99 percent black. Officials instituted a desegregation plan in 1965, but the situation barely changed. Finally, the NAACP brought the case to court on behalf of James Swann, a six-year-old student, and other families. A district court ruled that the school system was discriminatory and that residential housing patterns contributed to the unjust situation.

In 1971, *Swann v. Charlotte-Mecklenburg Board of Education* wound its way to the U.S. Supreme Court, which again showed its strong support for school desegregation. It declared that segregation was unconstitutional even if it was caused by geographic proximity rather than by an intent to segregate.

The court held that "the first remedial responsibility of school authorities is to eliminate invidious racial distinctions. . . . Normal administrative practice should then produce schools of like quality, facilities, and staffs." The court added: "An optional majority-to-minority transfer provision has long been recognized as a useful part of a desegregation plan, and to be effective such arrangement must provide the transferring student free transportation and available space in the school to which he desires to move."

In *Swann*, the court declared its support of desegregation in other ways, including: ". . . local authorities and district courts must see to it that future school construction and abandonment are not used and do not serve to perpetuate or reestablish a dual system." With this ruling, the court's support for desegregation reached a zenith, as future decisions—at least those beginning in 1974—would chip away at the gains of integrationists.

To rectify the situation in Charlotte, the court required students to be bused to achieve racial balance—and not just to another part of the city, but to schools outside Charlotte's city limits. Known as area-wide busing, this form of court-enforced desegregation could have turned the nation on its head. Suburbs such as Cicero, Illinois, were vehement about keeping African Americans out of their communities. One can only imagine the uproar if black students were bused en masse to the public schools of that suburb and those like it.

But in Charlotte and Mecklenburg County, the system largely worked—even though whites initially resisted it. Judge James B. McMillan, the federal judge who first ordered deseg-regation in Charlotte, was hanged in effigy. And attorney Julius L. Chambers, who argued for desegregation, endured bombings of his home and office.

The school system desegregated in several ways. At the elementary school level, black schools were paired with white schools; black students were transferred to the correspond-ing white school and vice versa. At the junior high and high school level, black students were bused to white schools from outlying areas.

There was one noteworthy exception. White students from the well-off Eastover neighborhood of Charlotte were bused to the predominantly black West Charlotte High School. Such a decision could have had explosive repercussions, but school officials came up with ways to make the plan more acceptable to whites. They redrew the boundaries of West Charlotte to include more middle-class black students, and they added new educational programs to the high school.

The first whites to attend West Charlotte High School are directed to classes by an African American assistant principal, Leroy Miller, in Charlotte, North Carolina, in September 1970.

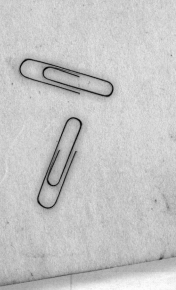

An estimated 1,700 whites stage a protest rally in downtown Charlotte, North Carolina, against the court-ordered desegregation plan in 1970.

GIVE
THE
PEOPLE
POWER
MY KidS
"Ain'T"
Bussin'
J.B.
McMILLIAN
IMPEACH
"BIG"
MAC

Many white parents also liked the high schools' "tracking" system. High-performing students took high-track classes. These tended to be the white students, so as a result Charlotte had segregation within the high schools. A 1981-82 survey of English classes found that "in this district acclaimed for its desegregation successes, relatively few black students experienced a genuinely desegregated education, even in its showcase high school."

The tracking system, which to this day leads to intrasegregated high schools throughout the country, was the only major blemish of the Charlotte plan. In 1981, a *Charlotte Observer* editorial declared, "Schools are no longer black or white, but are simply schools. As a result, the racial composition of surrounding areas is not as critical as it once was. The center city and its environs are a healthy mixture of black and white neighborhoods."

Charlotte experienced relatively little white flight, largely because white families had nowhere to go. The desegregation plan extended throughout the city's outlying area, so families would have had to move great distances to avoid integration.

Richmond, Virginia

In Richmond, the state capital, schools and neighborhoods remained segregated through the 1960s. Recalled Jennifer Turnage, who was born in 1958, "I lived in an all-black neighborhood and went to an all-black elementary school. The only white people I came in contact with were on television." To dismantle segregation, U.S. District Judge Robert Mehrige, in the 1971 case *Bradley v. Richmond School Board*, ordered a citywide busing program.

Many white families didn't want to accept their new intracity busing system. A classic photograph reveals white Richmond students standing in a pickup truck that says

Robert R. Merhige Jr. in 1977

"No Busing" on its side. The students raise homemade signs that say "Freedom of Choice Forever: No We Are Not Going" and "If We Are Bused, We Won't Go."

But the busing program was instituted in the fall of 1971. Parents and students—black and white—groaned about the hardships: long bus rides, the separation of siblings, and the inability of the students to participate in after-school activities. Unlike the Charlotte plan, whites could avoid desegregation by moving to the suburbs. Many did, leading to substantial white flight.

In early 1972, Judge Mehrige responded to white flight. Not only would he continue busing in Richmond, but he would extend it to the suburban counties so that whites would have nowhere to flee. White students from the counties would be bused to black schools in the city, and black Richmond students would be bused to white schools. Mehridge called it the "only remedy promising success," but many thought his decision was outrageous.

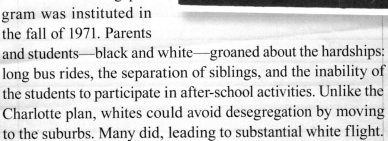

Mehrige's decision was appealed, and the U.S. Fourth Circuit Court of Appeals overturned it in a near-unanimous decision. The U.S. Supreme Court then upheld the appeals court's ruling. While the high court had increased its support of busing in previous decisions, it began its retreat on the matter with the Richmond case.

While desegregation and busing continued *within* Richmond, whites continued to move to the suburbs. According to Turnage, the integrated city schools fell short of what idealists had envisioned. "Teachers started placing more emphasis on white kids—white kids excelling," she recalled. "I remember when I got to high school, I was put in an advanced English class and the black teacher I had paid more attention to the white kids. She praised the white kids more than she did us. For the most part, we sat in the back of the room."

Nashville, Tennessee

Busing became a major issue in many large cities in the 1970s, including Nashville, Tennessee. Because of Nashville's inability to fully desegregate following the 1954 *Brown* decision, Federal Judge L. Clure Morton in 1971 ordered forced busing throughout the school district, which encompassed not just Nashville but all of Davidson County. In this sense, the plan was similar to the one in Charlotte.

In Nashville, the opposition was intense. In March 1971, 1,500 parents gathered at Nashville's War Memorial Auditorium to hear white Metro Council member Casey Jenkins denounce that city's court-ordered plan. "Busing to create racial balance is an ugly creature, busing is unconstitutional . . . busing deprives us of our freedom of expression, of our freedom of choice, of our property rights and our civil rights," he said.

As in other busing decisions, Nashville's mayor resented the federal court's ruling because the city couldn't afford what the judge wanted them to do. To fulfill Judge Morton's order, Nashville had to come up with more than $2 million to buy 127 new buses for the fall term. "We don't have the money," fumed Mayor Beverly Briley. "I don't know where such an additional amount of money can come from . . . there is no money in the budget for this purpose," Briley added, "The courts should stay out of education, and education should stay out of the courts."

Unlike in Charlotte, the Nashville plan was not deemed a success. Many parents sent their children to the numerous private schools that opened in the 1960s and '70s. Moreover, others moved out of Davidson County to avoid being part of the desegregation plan. There was a whole lot of busing, and much inconvenience because of it, but the city did not achieve the goals of the plan: racial diversity and improved education.

Pasadena, California

Some of the desegregation orders were outside of the South. Pasadena, California, a traditionally wealthy and conservative suburb of Los Angeles that's known for its annual Rose Bowl Parade, was targeted in 1970. In the 1960s, the city had become two separate communities: one well-to-do and largely white and the other African American. In 1970, U.S. District Judge Manuel Real ordered the city to desegregate its schools. In this case, it was a one-way street: Pasadena's black students would be bused to that city's white schools.

Once again, the decision largely backfired. Most whites hated the Pasadena Plan, and the white flight began. From 1970 to 1973, the percentage of white students in Pasadena's public junior highs and high schools fell from 58 percent to 50 percent. Opposition was so strong that Pasadena voters elected an antibusing majority to the school board in 1973.

By decade's end, only 29 percent of Pasadena's public school students were white. Numerous private schools opened their doors during the decade.

White educator William Bibiani said that whites encouraged others of their race to avoid the mixed-race public schools. "When I was looking for a house here," he said, "several realtors subtly, or not so subtly, hinted that I ought to consider private schools."

School board member Katie Nack recalled that parents of both races no longer valued the education of Pasadena's public schools. "It was not only white flight, but bright flight," she said. "We lost some of our best minority students too, because of fear of what might happen and because of relaxation of educational standards."

Yet, like with every other desegregation program, there were two sides to the story. Andre Coleman, a black first-grader in 1970, recalled that busing improved racial harmony—at least among parents in his desegregated school's parking lot. At first, he said, "the black parents and the white parents didn't intermingle, but slowly they began to speak to each other and laugh and talk."

Denver, Colorado

In 1973 and '74, the U.S. Supreme Court made two important decisions related to desegregation. The first one, *Keyes v. School District No. 1, Denver*, was significant because it concerned a school district that did not have a history of state-imposed segregation—that is, it was not a school district in a southern state or border state. The court ruled that the Denver, Colorado, school board "by use of various techniques such as the manipulation of student attendance zones, school site selection, and a neighborhood school policy created or maintained racially or ethnically (or both racially and ethnically) segregated schools."

According to education historians Stephen J. Caldas and Carl L. Bankston, "The Keyes case thus opened up school systems across the entire United States to legal desegregation action." While court-ordered desegregation mandates were mostly in the South prior to 1973, the trend shifted greatly after that year. Major desegregation plans would unfold in such cities as Boston (1974), Dayton, Ohio (1976), Milwaukee, Wisconsin (1976), Buffalo, New York (1976), and Wilmington, Delaware (1978).

Beginning in 1974, the Supreme Court made a series of rulings that were deemed antibusing. Republican president Richard Nixon had much to do with the swing. After taking office in 1969, Nixon appointed three Supreme Court justices and one chief justice, the conservative Warren Burger. Nixon was strongly opposed to busing, and it affected his selection of justices. When talking to Attorney General John Mitchell in 1971 about replacing a retiring liberal justice, Nixon said that the new justice must fall "within the definition of conservative" and that "he must be against busing, and against forced housing integration. Beyond that, he can do what he pleases."

President Richard Nixon in 1971

Detroit, Michigan

In 1974, the Supreme Court decided an extremely important desegregation case, *Milliken v. Bradley*, with William Milliken being the governor of Michigan. In Detroit and other major northern and eastern cities, whites had fled to the suburbs in droves in the 1960s and early '70s—largely due to the allure of the suburbs but in part because of the race riots of the late 1960s. Since suburban homes were relatively expensive, and because suburbanites were often unwelcoming to African Americans, the suburbs were predominantly white. The urban areas became largely black.

Although segregation was not legally imposed in Detroit and other northern and eastern cities, the separation of the races was clearly evident. Black students who attended public schools in the deteriorating city of Detroit unquestionably received an education inferior to those in the thriving suburbs.

A district court, recognizing this injustice, ordered a massive metropolitan-area busing plan in order to achieve greater racial parity. The busing plan would involve public school students in Detroit and fifty-three outlying school districts. White suburbanites were outraged. They claimed that they had worked hard to move to the suburbs and send their kids to good schools. The case was appealed to the U.S. Supreme Court and decided on July 25, 1974.

The court shot down the district court's desegregation plan. Specifically, the Supreme Court ruled that with "no showing of significant violation by the 53 outlying school districts and no evidence of any interdistrict violation or effect," the plan was "wholly impermissible."

The decision made headlines across the country. If the Supreme Court had approved the plan, it could have opened the door to city-to-suburbs busing in many American metropolises. The costs would have been enormous, and it would have led to major changes and disruptions in millions of Americans' lives.

The plan likely would have passed if President Nixon hadn't nominated four Republican justices. In fact, all four voted with the majority on a decision that narrowly passed (5-4). It could be said that the president had decided this Supreme Court case.

Two judges strongly opposed the decision. Justice William Douglas stated that "Michigan, by one device or another, has, over the years, created black school districts and white school districts," and that "the schools are segregated by race and . . . the black schools are not only 'separate' but 'inferior.'" He lamented how the state could now wash "its hands of its own creations."

Justice Thurgood Marshall, the legendary attorney who had won the *Brown* case in 1954, lamented the continuation of segregation, meaning predominantly white suburban schools and black city schools. "[U]nless our children begin to learn together," he wrote, "there is little hope that our people will ever learn to live together."

The issue of busing was dividing not just the Supreme Court but communities as well. In 1974, it would tear Boston apart.

Buses arrive at South Boston High School as classes
resume at the racially troubled institution in
January 1975. Police were on hand to provide
protection as black students arrived.

chapter 4

The Fury in Boston

In April 1945, two years before he integrated Major League Baseball with the Brooklyn Dodgers, Jackie Robinson tried out for the Boston Red Sox. With only team officials in the stands at Fenway Park that day, someone yelled, "Get those niggers off the field!"

Despite his Hall of Fame talent, Robinson wasn't signed by Boston. In fact, the Red Sox—who acquired the reputation as a racist organization—became the last big-league team to field an African American: Pumpsie Green in 1959.

For generations, Boston and Massachusetts were known as, conversely, hotbeds of both liberalism and racism. Though the first colony to make slavery legal, in 1641, Massachusetts became the epicenter for abolitionism. The state eventually earned the nicknamed "Taxachusetts" for its desire to heavily fund social programs. President John Kennedy and Senator Ted Kennedy, both from Boston, are liberal icons. Yet in the decades that followed World War II, the Irish in the large Boston neighborhoods of Charlestown and South Boston resented the increasing influx of African Americans into their communities.

The Irish at the time were a tight-knit, insular ethnic group. Wrote Irishman Thomas H. O'Connor in the book *South Boston*, the Irish believed that they "should stay with their own people . . . go to your own church . . . and marry your own kind." But as more and more black Americans entered the city in the postwar era, O'Connor wrote, Irish, Italians, "and other residents of traditionally white neighborhoods panicked as they thought of blacks taking their jobs, lowering the standards of their schools, bringing down property values, and adding to the danger of crime in the streets."

By the early 1970s, the racial problems intensified. In poor, working-class South Boston, the neighborhood was deteriorating. Unemployment was on the rise, adding to the competition for jobs between working-class whites and blacks. Undereducated whites had been more resentful than sympathetic to the demands of black leaders during the civil rights movement, and the aggressive nature of the Black Power movement intensified the hostility. Southies (as those in South Boston were called) complained that while Irish politicians had traditionally taken care of their people in Boston, the new Irish politicians were "limousine liberals"—high-minded progressives who championed black civil rights.

The conflicts reached a head with the fight over the state's Racial Imbalance Law, which had been passed in 1965. From that point up until 1973, the state board pushed Boston's school board for a plan to deal with its sixty-plus schools that were more than 50 percent black. Boston school officials refused, saying that housing patterns, not intentional segregation, caused the racial imbalance. They also reiterated that Boston had an open enrollment policy, which allowed students to enroll in any public school that had a vacancy. Moreover, they agreed to offer additional education programs for African American students within their current schools.

The conflict worsened in 1971, when the Boston School Committee refused the state's order to desegregate Lee Elementary School in the Dorchester neighborhood. The state board responded by withholding funds for the city, and the NAACP filed a lawsuit, *Morgan v. Hennigan*, against the school committee. U.S. District Judge W. Arthur Garrity Jr. presided over the case. A Harvard Law School grad and a former campaign worker for John F. Kennedy, Garrity was revered within the law profession. Yet he was about to become one of the most vilified judges in American history.

Garrity did not hand down his ruling until June 21, 1974. He declared that the Boston School Committee had "knowingly carried out a systematic program of segregation affecting all of the city's students, teachers, and school facilities and [had] intentionally brought about and maintained a dual school system."

Garrity accepted a racial-balancing plan created by the State Board of Education in which 17,000 Boston students would be bused to other schools in the city. It would go into effect at the beginning of the 1974-75 school year. Non-Boston educators, according to O'Connor, "drew a series of arcs across a map of the city in a mechanical fashion, cutting up the various districts in such a way that each school included the right proportion of black and white children."

The State Board of Education's most alarming decision was to exchange white students from the heavily Irish South Boston with African American students from the black neighborhood of Roxbury. The state board members were setting up a war between the neighborhoods, with schoolchildren as the soldiers.

On September 9, three days before the school year began, more than 8,000 angry antibusing protesters gathered at city hall. When U.S. senator Ted Kennedy, a supporter of civil rights and the busing program, addressed the crowd, they roared with anger. Shouts, curses, tomatoes, and eggs flew through the air. At one point, those in the crowd turned their backs on Kennedy in unison. One woman punched him. One man tried to kick him. Reporters recorded just some of the vile insults:

Senator Ted Kennedy (right, looking down) waits to speak to the thousands of protesters in Boston, on September 9, 1974. Kennedy did not get to speak to them but was whisked off the platform when the crowd started chanting insults at him.

"You're a disgrace to the Irish."

"Why don't you put your one-legged son on a bus for Roxbury."

"Let your daughter get bused there so she can get raped."

"Why don't you let them shoot you like they shot your two brothers."

When Kennedy retreated to the Federal Building, the mob pounded on the glass doors until they broke. "It was great," said Pat Ranese, an aide to antibusing leader Louise Day Hicks. "It's about time the politicians felt the anger of the people. We've been good for too long. They'd pat us on the backs, and we'd go home. No more."

On the first day of school, Thursday, September 12, 20,000 of the Boston public schools' 87,000 students were scheduled to take the bus. Some would travel several blocks; others several miles. Out of protest (a planned boycott) and fear, only 124 (fifty-six black) out of 1,300 students showed up at South Boston High School, where graffitists wrote "Kill niggers" and other epithets on the exterior walls. Southies indeed went on the attack. A hostile crowd chucked rocks at several school buses that carried black children. They shattered the buses' windows, and they injured nine black high school students.

Boston would be called the Little Rock of the North because of this reaction to integration. In 1957, President Dwight Eisenhower had to call in the National Guard to escort nine black students to Central High School amid a hostile white mob. The scene was eerily similar on this day. As a police escort led her bus to South Boston High School that day, African American student Phyllis Ellison felt frightened but important—just like the members of the Little Rock Nine. She recalled:

Well, when we started up the hill you could hear people saying, "Niggers go home." There were signs, they had made a sign saying, "Black people stay out. We don't want any niggers in our school." And there were people on the corners holding bananas like we were apes, monkeys. . . . So at that time it did frighten me somewhat, but I was more determined then to get inside South Boston High School. . . . I felt like I was making history, because that was the first year of desegregation and all the controversies and conflicts at that time. I felt that the black students there were making history.

Boston reporter Alan Lupo remembered the "growl" of the white crowd of five hundred demonstrators outside South Boston High School. He studied the faces:

What I saw was black kids looking at where they were being bused and being disappointed. Black kids smiling as if to be cocky but really nervous. Blacks walking as if to taunt the white kids but, I think, really scared. White families looking, with perhaps a combination of hatred and fear, and other whites looking with no hatred but fear and curiosity. Children looking with ignorance and awe. Their hands being held by parents who had been through a lot of hell in their white lives and were looking at a change that they couldn't understand. It was a pitiful sight for everybody.

Boston Mayor Kevin White, who was known for trying to satisfy all factions of his city, insisted on just a small police presence on opening day. But after the attacks and injuries to students, an army of police officers arrived in South Boston the next day. Throughout the school year and beyond, South Boston would resemble a police state.

Antibusing proponents wanted to march in South Boston that weekend, but the mayor wouldn't allow it. Instead, some three hundred rioted on Monday, damaging phones and benches at an MBTA station and assaulting black citizens. Two dozen people were arrested. Day after day, tempers flared at South Boston High. Other schools saw sporadic violence, including Hyde Park High School and Jamaica Plain High School, where a shot was fired through a door.

Tracy Amalfitano worried every day about her children getting to school safely. She would get nervous, and then she'd get mad. "I said, Why would anyone interfere with my right to send my kids to school? . . . Many days I would come home and I would think about all the liberals that got on the buses and went south for sit-ins and boycotts, and I really would come home and wonder, Where were they now?"

Peg Smith, an antibusing leader in the Charlestown neighborhood, felt that her rights had been violated—that the federal courts had overstepped their bounds. "I want my freedom back," she said. "They took my freedom. They tell me where my kids have to go to school. This is like living in Russia. Next they'll tell you where to shop."

As in southern cities in the post-*Brown* era, some whites created alternative schools in Boston. During evenings, they brought the students to empty rooms at veterans posts and yacht clubs. Some teachers volunteered their time to educate them.

In other cities, opponents of desegregation usually resigned themselves to their fate. Not in Boston. The protests and violence continued. Whites, blacks, and police battled in Columbia Point. On October 4, thousands of antibusers marched on "National Boycott Day." Some three hundred of them went to Garrity's home in suburban Wellesley, where they chanted in front of a line of police.

A portion of the crowd that gathered in Wellesley outside the home of U.S. District Judge W. Arthur Garrity. They were protesting the forced busing of Boston schoolchildren.

At the Rabbit Inn bar in South Boston, police and locals clashed violently on successive nights, with numerous injuries. In October, a mass rock-throwing fracas in Mission Hill resulted in thirty-eight injuries. Mayor White pleaded with Judge Garrity to call in federal marshals to support his overtaxed police force, but Garrity refused, saying it was Boston's responsibility. President Gerald Ford showed his support for the antibusers, saying in a press conference that "I have consistently opposed forced busing to achieve racial balance as a solution to quality education. . . ." The president did put the Eighty-second Airborne Division on standby in case the situation in Boston got out of hand.

Across the city, antibusing violence subsided somewhat throughout the fall, and many boycotters returned to school. The uprising in South Boston improved but still continued. There were sixteen assaults on teachers at South Boston High in October and seven in November. Whites continued to verbally assault black students. Police patrolled not just the outside grounds but the hallways, stairwells, and cafeteria. Metal detectors and snipers became part of the story.

An exasperated Mayor White compared his city to the capital of strife-torn Northern Ireland. "Sometimes when I look out this window," he reportedly said to an aide, "I see Belfast out there."

Antibusers staged a school boycott on November 5, election day, and they planned rallies that each attracted several thousand people. When a black student stabbed a white student on December 7, more than two hundred white students walked out at Hyde Park High School.

As the school year wound down, close to a hundred police officers still patrolled South Boston High. The teachers at the school were at wit's end. At the close of the last day of classes, "Hallelujah" was played over the public address system.

A police marksman and a lookout watch from the roof of Charlestown High School as school buses arrive bringing African American students to the all-white area in Boston on September 8, 1975. The school was integrated for the first time under Phase II of the desegregation plan.

After a year of such resistance, many thought Judge Garrity would back off his desegregation plan—for personal reasons if nothing else. Throughout the school year his home and office remained under twenty-four-hour guard. But Garrity actually intensified the desegregation program. As the 1975-76 school year approached, he rolled out Phase II of his desegregation plan. In this plan, up to 25,000 Boston students would be bused—7,000 more than the previous school year.

While reviled through much of Boston, Garrity had the U.S. Commission on Civil Rights on his side. The commissioners charged the Boston School Committee with pursuing a "deliberate policy of minimal compliance," which they said encouraged community resistance. They also criticized Mayor White for being ambivalent about enforcing the law. "Eighty percent of the people in Boston are against busing," the mayor responded. "If Boston were a sovereign state, busing would be cause for a revolution."

In preparation for the upcoming school year, Garrity ordered every neighborhood to establish a multiracial council to facilitate local desegregation. He even solicited the aid of Boston's many colleges and universities, asking them to help Boston's schools improve their educational programs. The police department got involved by assigning 1,600 officers to the opening day of school. Six hundred National Guardsmen were on call.

Boston councilwoman Louise Day Hicks, a matronly looking attorney, formed an organization to counter Garrity: Restore Our Alienated Rights (ROAR). Hicks struck a chord with Boston's working-class mothers when she cried, "They shall not take our children from us." Boston, she said, was not a city of well-established whites out to continue the oppression of African Americans. It was, she said, a city of ethnic enclaves: Chinese in Chinatown, Italians in the North End, blacks in Roxbury, and Irish in South Boston. That a federal judge would turn the city inside-out to serve just one of these groups, she felt, was deplorable.

"We're frightened," said ROAR co-founder Fran Johnnene. "We're locked in. People see their neighborhood threatened, and they're trapped there. What else could that mean but they'll fight back?"

Charlestown mothers and children march in opposition to school busing on September 9, 1975. The neighborhood high school was in its second day of desegregation.

With Garrity intensifying busing for the 1975-76 school year, ROAR responded with one of the most bizarre protest marches America had ever seen. That September, Hicks led a parade of three hundred white mothers down the streets of the Charlestown neighborhood. The women wore housedresses and curlers and pushed baby carriages, and they prayed with their rosaries as they walked. Why?

"We are asking God for relief because He's the only one that's listening to us," protester Pat Russell told a reporter.

"That's right," said a white man who was watching and drinking a beer. "No niggers."

ROAR members did not view themselves as racist but as victims. However, many Americans viewed them as militant bigots. "The parents are the cause of what's going on because they are teaching their kids to be against black people," said African American Gretchen Jones, who in September 1974 became the first black student to step off the bus at South Boston High.

Whites of South Boston and Charlestown sometimes felt that everyone was against them. Seething with anger, many of them acted out violently. On at least one occasion, whites hurled Molotov cocktails (homemade gasoline bombs) at police. Most of the officers were working-class whites like themselves, and many were Irish, yet antibusers viewed them as symbols of oppression. "These people feel like their town is being occupied by a foreign army," said Roberta Delaney of Charlestown. "It's enforcing a law that is not theirs." In South Boston, whites poured oil on a steep street, hoping that police motorcycles would skid down the pavement and crash. Fortunately, the "prank" was not successful.

Newsweek described seventeen-year-old Steven Fitzgerald of Southie as looking like an altar boy. But behind the innocent face was a heart that had gone cold. "If you're going to hit a nigger," he said, "you might as well take his wallet too.

A white student rides the bus with her black schoolmates to South Boston High School.

That way the cops get you for assault or robbery—not for violating his civil rights."

As the busing crisis dragged through its second year, many families couldn't take it anymore. George Bolanes, a Boston police officer, lived in the white working-class neighborhood of Roslindale. When the new school year started, his nine-year-old son Douglas was to be bused into Dorchester, known as a black ghetto. "I'd go into Dorchester," Bolanes said, "but I don't want my son to go." Thus, Bolanes decided to move to the suburbs. "I've thrown in the towel," he said. "This prob-lem will never be solved."

Garrity had ordered desegregation even though he had known there would be white flight, and there was. Many families moved to the suburbs or enrolled their children in private or parochial schools. From 1974 to 1984, the ratio of white students in Boston's public schools dropped from 57 percent to less than 27 percent, while the black student population rose from 34 percent to 48 percent. In terms of raw numbers, the results were startling: the number of white students dropped from 53,593 to 15,257.

In 1984, Garrity retained jurisdiction over the city's schools, and busing was still mandated. Yet with so many whites gone, the effort was becoming futile. "The racial balance plan is mathematically impossible to carry out," said John R. Coakley, who oversaw pupil assignment. "We are rapidly reaching the point where white enrollment is so small that the arithmetic of the case is losing its sense."

During that period, the violence cooled down substantially. Said Thomas Atkins, president of the Boston chapter of the NAACP. "The sustained guerrilla warfare conducted several years ago has given way to an attitude of 'I don't like it, but it's the law.'"

Many people didn't like it, including most African Americans. In a 1980 poll published in the *Boston Globe*, 80 percent of whites and the same number of blacks agreed that tax money should be spent on local school improvements rather than busing.

The overall result of Boston's busing program was mixed. On the plus side, Garrity's plan opened the doors for more minority teachers. In addition, the number of Boston high school graduates who went on to college rose from 41 percent to 62 percent (the trend toward college education was on the rise throughout the country).

"The desegregation order was a blessing to the school system," said John O'Bryant, who in 1977 became the first African American elected to the Boston School Committee. "The school system was in such a state of decline that, in essence, what happened was that the court order set up mechanisms whereby all schools were monitored, not just for integration but also for the level of the academic programs."

Not everyone shared O'Bryant's optimism. The annual high school dropout rate skyrocketed over the rest of the century, and most of Boston's public high schools had math and reading scores that were below the national average.

Of course, the upheaval caused emotional hardships for thousands of Bostonians. "A lot of people have been unnecessarily hurt," Edward J. Doherty, president of the teachers union, said in 1984. "The court orders and busing have been a dismal failure. My own daughter, who is in the seventh grade, is attending her fifth school because of closings and reassignments."

Though busing was intended to help young African Americans, it also "took away the community feeling we had for our neighborhood schools," said Gwendolyn Collins-Stevens of Roxbury, "the feeling of 'It's our school and we love it.'"

"When schools were segregated, they were rich in other ways," said Angela Paige Cook, founder of Paige Academy, a private school in Roxbury. "Before busing, parents, teachers, and students often lived in the same community, attended the same churches, and shopped in the same stores. There were more positive role models for the kids in those days. When you destroy a community infrastructure, you no longer have those role models."

To take the edge off forced busing, Boston established twenty-two magnet schools by 1984. Such public schools, which became popular throughout the country, were meant to attract students from all across the city. Magnet schools, which students have to test into, often specialize in a certain subject, such as math or the arts. One of the goals of magnet schools is to give students in poorer neighborhoods a chance to attend a good school.

Yet despite the emergence of the magnet schools, forced busing remained. For more than a decade, Garrity ruled over the Boston school system like a puppeteer. In 1985, Boston school superintendent Robert Spillane—the eighth person in ten years to hold that position—resigned out of frustration. Spillane said that Garrity "had a paternalistic mentality that all goodness and all knowledge flows from the federal court."

On September 3, 1985, Garrity finally abandoned his authority over the Boston Public Schools, handing the reins to the Massachusetts Board of Education. "I'll miss it," Garrity said, adding that the experience was "rewarding and inspiring."

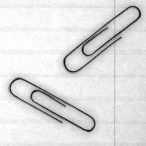

The United States
Capitol building

chapter 5

Battles on Capitol Hill

In the midst of the Boston crisis, Michael Novak of the Rockefeller Foundation called busing the "Vietnam of the 1970s"—a controversial, polarizing issue that was tearing the nation apart.

Poll results supported Novak's claim. A 1976 Roper Poll asked the following question: "Suppose a candidate took stands that you agreed with on all but one of these issues. Which one issue on the list would be most likely to turn you away from him if you disagreed with his stand on the issue?" Thirteen percent said abortion, which was extremely controversial in the mid-1970s due to the 1973 *Roe v. Wade* decision. Twenty percent said inflation, which had been a whopping 9.2 percent in 1975. But neither of those issues beat out busing, which topped the list at 22 percent.

As they watched the Boston fiasco unfold on their evening news, more and more Americans turned against mandated busing. In a 1976 Harris poll, 81 percent of whites opposed the busing of schoolchildren to achieve racial balance, and only 9 percent supported it. Among African Americans—the group that busing proponents were trying to help—51 percent opposed it and only 38 percent were for it.

With the busing issue so heated, and with public opinion so against it, politicians scrambled to voice their opposition. They understood that they would never get reelected on a probusing platform. A 1974 *U.S. News & World Report* issue featured the cover headline "Mood of America." In the issue, a reporter gave U.S. senator Joe Biden (D-DE) the chance to share his views on busing. Biden said:

> Examining the concepts we used to rationalize busing six or seven years ago, they now seem to me to be profoundly racist. Busing is harmful for several reasons:
>
> First, busing, in effect, codifies the concept that a black is inferior to a white by saying, "The only way you can cut it educationally is if you're with whites." I think that's a horrible concept. It implies that blacks have no reason to be proud of their [heritage] and their own culture. . . .
>
> Second, busing violates the cardinal rule that the American people pose for their elected officials. They'll forgive our greed. They expect it. But the one thing they don't expect—and won't tolerate—is not using good old common sense. The reason, in my opinion, why there's such a vociferous reaction to busing today in both black and white communities is that we're not using common sense. Common sense says to the average American: "The idea that you make me part

Senator Joe Biden in 1975

of a racial percentage instead of a person in a classroom is asinine."

In addition, busing also is damaging because it spends on transportation money that could be better spent on new textbooks and other educational improvements.

The reporter asked Biden what his white constituents were saying.

I firmly believe the overwhelming majority of white people have no objection whatever to their child sitting with a black child, eating lunch with

a black child—all the things that were the basis
for the racist movement in the past. But it makes
no sense to them that they can't send their child
to the school that's two blocks down the street.
And what this results in is heightened racial tension. You get whites saying: 'I know why it's
happening. It's those goldarned civil-rights people. It's those damn liberals.' Then, after there's
turmoil, with school days missed, teachers not
showing up, it degenerates into: 'It's those blacks.'

In Washington, the busing issue had all branches of government on edge. Republican Edward H. Levi, a highly respected
figure, served as attorney general under President Gerald Ford.
In June 1976, Levi indicated that judges had gone too far in
their busing orders. He said that any judge who "believes that
his duty is to achieve a racial balance in every school is reaching for a remedy which is beyond the Constitution."

President Ford, in the midst of a reelection campaign that
summer, knew that he had to address the issue. His Republican
competitor for president, Ronald Reagan was stating publicly how he would deal with busing. "As President," Reagan
declared, "I would propose to Congress legislation—in keeping with the Fourteenth Amendment—that would eliminate
forced busing." Another option, Reagan, said, was the passage
of a constitutional amendment to eliminate it.

Ford listened to the National Institute of Research, which
delivered its findings to the president. The institute had discov-
ered the following: Desegregation did not reduce achievement
scores of whites, but it did increase achievement scores of
blacks—slightly. White flight often accompanied desegregation, but the degree of white flight varied considerably
depending on the city.

The Ford administration wasn't sure what to do. In May 1976, they planned to ask the Supreme Court to address the constitutionality of the Boston busing plan and to reconsider the 1971 *Swann v. Charlotte-Mecklenburg* case. (In *Swann*, the court had ruled that segregation was unconstitutional even if it was caused by housing patterns rather than intentional school segregation.) Attorney General Levi, however, dissuaded the president from moving in this direction.

President Gerald Ford talks with reporters at the White House in 1976.

In June 1976, Ford urged three more proposals. First, the president pressed Levi to draft a bill in which forced desegregation could occur only after local governments and school boards had deliberately caused school segregation. For example, the government would take action if local officials had redrawn school district boundaries for the benefit of white families. The president's second proposal was to limit forced desegregation to the specific schools where segregation existed—not over the entire city. Later that June, the White House proposed another plan: limit the duration of court-ordered busing to five years.

Not surprisingly, Ford was criticized from all corners. Depending on the source, he was either too soft, too hard, or too indecisive on the issue of busing. Boston antibusing leader Louise Day Hicks said about the five-year plan, "Give us three more years and we'll have a nonwhite city. Five years is too late for Boston."

The Leadership Conference on Civil Rights insisted that desegregation efforts continue. The conference implored the president "to cease judicial and legislative efforts" to restrict "the scope of remedies for unconstitutional segregation" and "to issue a national call for obedience to the rule of law."

A group of educators, researchers, and city officials submitted this statement to the president: "We have come to believe that the premises on which the case for court-ordered busing have been built are faulty. . . . We deplore the assumption that neighborhood schools cannot, if they are black, attain high levels of excellence. But we believe strongly that opportunity to choose freely to send one's children to schools outside the neighborhood should be open to every family."

Despite President Ford's desire to do something about busing, neither Congress nor the Supreme Court took major steps to alter the practice. Ford lost his bid for reelection in

November 1976 to civil rights supporter Jimmy Carter. As the nation tired of Carter's policies, conservative politicians gained influence in Washington. In 1978, the Supreme Court ruled, in *University of California Regents v. Bakke*, that colleges and universities could not use racial quotas in their admissions process. In other words, a college could not say that 10 percent of its incoming freshmen had to be African American. That would be, the court believed, unfair to the non-black students who had better grades and test scores.

Although this landmark case seemingly had nothing to do with forced busing, it did prove again that the Supreme Court had changed its attitude toward race-related school issues over the past decade. Some black rights activists did tie the two together: If black children were given an inferior public school education, and then were not cut a break when it came to college admissions, how would they ever rise above?

Carter himself would support desegregation efforts. He appointed civil rights officials who supported desegregation, and during his administration the Justice Department filed desegregation suits. One such suit resulted in a massive busing plan in Indianapolis, Indiana.

In President Carter's final months in office, Congress passed a bill to curb busing: While private organizations could bring suit to require forced desegregation, the U.S. Justice Department would be prohibited from doing so. Carter vetoed the bill.

But when Ronald Reagan became president on January 20, 1981, desegregation supporters knew their cause was doomed—at least at the federal level. The conservative president would focus his eight-year presidency on stimulating the economy, winning the Cold War against the Soviet Union through military buildup, and slashing the "waste" of social programs. Reagan strongly opposed forced desegregation and

President Jimmy Carter and wife Rosalynn meet President-elect Ronald Reagan and his wife Nancy, right, at the North Portico of the White House on January 20, 1981.

was no friend of the civil rights movement. He said of the civil rights brass, "[S]ome of those leaders are doing very well [financially] leading organizations based on keeping alive the feeling that they're victims of prejudice."

In 1981, Assistant Attorney General for Civil Rights William Bradford Reynolds set the tone for the new administration's busing policy. "[C]ompulsory busing of students in order to achieve racial balance in the public schools is not an acceptable remedy," he declared. "[This position] has been endorsed by the president, vice president, the secretary of education, and me."

In the first few months of 1981, the Reagan administration successfully pushed Congress to rescind the Emergency School Aid Act of 1982. This act had provided federal funds to state and local governments that were forced to desegregate, since the costs of doing so were high (for example, buying new buses). The administration also successfully campaigned Congress to slash federal funding of Desegregation Assistance Centers.

The Reagan administration shut off research on how desegregation could be more effective, and it took control of the U.S. Civil Rights Commission. In eight years under Reagan, the Justice Department did not file one desegregation lawsuit. In fact, it looked for ways to reverse desegregation cases. In 1983, the Justice Department asked the U.S. Supreme Court to restrict busing in Nashville, Tennessee. It also supported the dismantling of segregation in other cities, including Norfolk, Virginia.

As the authors of *Dismantling Desegregation* stated, "During this period, the Justice Department insisted that the plans were failures, unfair to whites and to local school systems. The plans should be seen as temporary punishments only, and districts should be allowed to return to segregated neighborhood schools."

President Reagan and his Republican successor, George H. W. Bush, appointed six justices to the U.S. Supreme Court, leading to conservative decisions in the 1980s and beyond that made school desegregation more difficult

As Washington grappled with the issue over the years, Americans in general became more accepting of forced busing. But busing still had profound effects on families across the land, including the Johnson family in Lansing, Michigan.

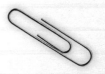

Motorcycle police escort buses to a school in Boston in 1974.

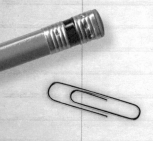

The Buses Keep Rolling

As a child in the 1960s and early '70s, Earvin Johnson loved his black, working-class neighborhood in Lansing, Michigan. Many of the men worked for General Motors or one of the company's subsidiaries. Earvin, the future basketball superstar known as "Magic," knew many of the kids in the neighborhood. He saw them at church, school, the local Boys' Club, and on the Main Street basketball courts near his house.

For Earvin, it was an idyllic childhood—until busing entered the equation. In 1974, Johnson was one of the African American kids from his area who were selected to be bused to Everett High School (grades ten to twelve), a mostly white public school several miles away. Earvin did not want to go.

Earvin Johnson in 2007

"I was upset," Johnson said. "I wanted to go to Sexton. All the dudes I played with went to Sexton. I went to every Sexton game. I was a Sexton man, and then they came up with this busing thing."

Earvin's older brothers, Quincy and Larry, had been bused to Everett and didn't like it. They had witnessed fights, brick throwing, and other racial incidents. Moreover, Larry had been cut from the Everett varsity basketball team, and he believed that race had much to do with it. Earvin wrote a letter to the school board, pleading to go to nearby Sexton, but his request was ignored. He had to attend Everett High School.

At Everett, recalled basketball coach George Fox, busing "was very controversial. Racial tension ran high. The white kids didn't want them there, and the black kids didn't want to be there."

For Johnson, trouble ensued during the team's first scrimmage. Time after time he was open for an easy basket, and the point guard—a white senior—did not pass him the ball. "Give it up!" Earvin finally blurted. "I was wide open three straight times." The player shoved Johnson and insulted him with a racial slur. The players soon resolved their differences, and "Magic" eventually led them to the state championship.

Earvin Johnson was just one of millions of Americans with stories to tell about busing. Desegregation affected families in numerous cities, including some of the largest in the nation.

Louisville, Kentucky

In Louisville, forced busing resulted in high drama. It all
started when the Sixth Circuit Court of Appeals ruled that
city-to-suburb busing (and vice versa) was permitted because
Louisville and Jefferson County had engaged in intentional
segregation, thus invalidating the ban on interdistrict busing
laid down in the *Milliken* decision. The U.S. Supreme Court
approved the appeals court's ruling, and busing began in
September 1975.

To many suburban whites, the busing plan was the worst
news possible. Not only would busing be intercity, but suburban white students would be bused into Louisville. And unlike
in other plans, in which the preponderance of bused students
were black, in the metro Louisville plan just as many suburban
white students would be bused to the city as black students to
the suburbs. Suburban communities were outraged.

Sensing a Boston-like reaction on Opening Day, U.S.
District Judge James F. Gordon declared that anyone who
attacked school buses would face federal prosecution. But citizens were defiant, and many of the scenes that took place in
Boston played out in Louisville. First came the mass protest
against busing: a gathering of 10,000 at the Kentucky State
Fairgrounds on September 3, the day before school began.

As in Boston, Opening Day saw large gatherings of protesters outside schools. At Fairdale High School in Louisville,
some 150 demonstrators tried to block eight buses filled with
black students. Families staged a boycott, with more than half
of the 130,000 Louisville/Jefferson County students staying
home. At Medora Elementary School in Louisville, eight-year-
old white student Timmy Hopewell sat bewilderedly in his
classroom, all alone. "I thought everybody must be sick," he
said.

A Kentucky State Police trooper stands guard as a bus rolls out of the Southern High School grounds in Louisville in September 1975.

On the first day of classes, black students bused to suburban schools feared what lay ahead. African American Leslie Lacy, a seventeen-year-old en route to a white school, wanted to make a U-turn. "I think I'll paint myself white and go back to Shawnee," she said.

On Friday evening, September 5, violence broke out in the white suburb of Valley Station. Driving en masse to a football game at Valley High School, drivers honked their horns to display their opposition to busing. One young driver parked his car in the middle of the road and ripped the hood off his own vehicle. When police arrived, people poured out of their cars and threw bottles and stones at the officers, calling them "Communists" and "pigs."

Local police, of course, had nothing to do with the busing decision, but as in Boston they served as scapegoats for an angry populace. The crowd swelled to more than 10,000, and people started bonfires on the highway. Police used tear gas to subdue the rioters and arrested numerous protesters.

News of the riot spread, prompting antibusing troublemakers to wreak havoc at other schools. At Southern High School in Louisville, they set two school buses on fire and attacked the windows and tires of forty more. "We don't want niggers in our schools," they chanted. In the suburbs, rioters looted stores and vented their anger on street signs. Hundreds of state troopers were called in to aid the county police force, and at 4 a.m. Governor Julian Carroll Overall called in the National Guard. Overall, fifty people were injured, and close to two hundred were arrested.

As in all other cities with busing, the violence simmered down over time and people adjusted to the new system—or opted out of it. Many white families either enrolled their children in private schools or moved to suburbs where busing wasn't mandated.

Integration also led to tension within Louisville-area schools, at least in the early years. One reporter noted in 1978, "Discipline problems have soared. White parents fear that the quality of education has declined, while black parents fear the loss of their community identity and institutions."

As was typical in integrated school systems, the aggregate test scores of black students did not approach the scores of white students. But there were signs of hope. Testing in the early 1980s revealed that black students' test scores did rise while white students' scores stayed the same. Moreover, some praised the metro-wide program for contributing to the desegregation of suburban neighborhoods, in part because some black families moved to neighborhoods in which their children were assigned to school.

Chicago, Illinois

In Chicago the school board instituted a limited busing program, along with the introduction of magnet schools, in 1967, but the plan did not prevent the city's schools from being highly segregated. In 1976, the state threatened to cut off all funding unless the city took a stronger initiative. The Chicago Board of Education responded with its "Access to Excellence" plan. The goal was to bus African American students from overcrowded, predominantly black schools in the inner city to "white" schools in the more affluent neighborhoods. But the program was voluntary, and in 1977 only one thousand black students chose to participate.

The South Side of Chicago had long been a hotbed of bigotry. In 1966, a protester chucked a rock that hit the head of Martin Luther King Jr., who said he had never seen such racial hatred, not even in the Deep South. On September 11, 1977, whites in a southwest Chicago neighborhood held a candlelight

Dr. Martin Luther King Jr. inside a South Side Chicago church where he opened a three-day campaign against alleged de facto segregation in the city's schools

vigil in protest of incoming black students. Whites picketed schools, and hundreds of students staged a walkout.

Since approximately 475,000 students (60 percent black, 22 percent white) attended Chicago public schools, the "Access to Excellence" plan had little impact. The U.S. Justice Department pressured the city, and eventually a compromise was reached. There would be no massive busing, but students at predominantly black and Hispanic schools would be offered compensatory education programs. Moreover, the Chicago School Board in 1981 limited white enrollment in a school to 70 percent.

By the 2000s, less than 10 percent of the city's students were white.

Wilmington, Delaware

In the 1970s, Wilmington adopted one of the most drastic desegregation plans in the nation—the busing of black city students to the suburbs and white suburban students to the city.

Early in the decade, the schools in Wilmington were predominantly black while those in the suburbs were mostly white. For several years, a busing plan would repeatedly be discussed, agreed upon, and then postponed. Long before a program was finally implemented, local citizens were on edge. "People are scared—there's no doubt about it," said Mayor John McLaughlin. White families so feared that their children would be bused that white enrollment in the suburban public schools plummeted.

"White parents don't want their children going to former all-black schools because they think the facilities are inferior," said Wendell Howell, president of the Wilmington School Board. "I once saw a white parent looking for rats and roaches and holes under a refrigerator when she came to visit one of our schools, and we have some of the finest facilities in the country."

The Wilmington busing program finally went into effect in September 1978. According to the highly controversial plan, black city students would be bused to predominantly white suburban schools for nine of their twelve years, while white suburban students would be bused to the city's black schools for three years each.

According to the *Washington Post* in 1977, "It's almost impossible to find anyone for busing" in Wilmington. As in other cities, even many African Americans—whom the plan was designed to help—were against it, particularly the nine years vs. three years aspect. "It was felt that poor kids shouldn't be forced to carry a disproportionate burden of desegregation on their shoulders," Howell said.

Although the Wilmington desegregation plan was revised in 1981, busing continued in the county until 2001. Over the last forty years, a high proportion of the area's families have opted for private, charter, and magnet schools—anything to avoid the standard public schools.

Beaumont, Texas

The events in Beaumont illustrate the severity of white reaction as well as how complicated busing plans could get.

From 1962 to 1974, desegregation was debated in the South Texas city. Finally, in 1975, a major plan was implemented. The two Beaumont high schools were combined into one massive learning facility, and attendance boundaries were redrawn for all schools.

More noteworthy was the case of South Park, a wealthy white district within Beaumont. In 1970, the federal government ordered the district to desegregate. Not only would black students be admitted to South Park High School, but between two to three hundred white South Park High students would be transferred to predominantly black Hebert High School. Immediately, white families began selling their homes. "Within 30 days, the neighborhoods were vacant and virtually every house for sale," said a lawyer for the South Park district. Only a hundred white students showed up for the first day of classes, and only ten remained in the school a month later.

In 1981, U.S. District Judge Robert Parker came up with a novel idea for desegregating the South Park school district: Ping-Pong balls. On a hot and humid morning in August, South Park School Superintendent Mike Taylor presided over a drum of five hundred plastic balls, half of them white and half yellow. Over a period of eleven hours, the drum was spun 8,000 times. Each spin determined which public school a South Park student would attend through eighth grade.

This "system" would ensure that South Park's schools would be integrated. But again, the citizens were upset. Outside the courthouse, mothers wept as they talked to reporters. A ten-year-old black child held up a sign that said "Go Home Feds!" Another sign read "We Are Not Ping-Pong Balls!"

Riverside, California

In 1965, Riverside became the first large city (with a population above 100,000) to totally desegregate its public schools. Researchers found several noteworthy effects of that city's busing experiment. Professor Harold Gerard and his colleagues observed that while the schools were desegregated, many black students were still marginalized in the classrooms.

Gerard found that the spirit of integration correlated with the success of the minority students. If white students were welcoming to the African American children, the latter performed better academically. But all too often the black students felt like outsiders in the classroom, even after several years. Gerard also found that black students suffered academically if the teacher was deprecating or patronizing. According to Gerard, desegregation was not enough to help minority students. A positive and welcoming learning environment was critically important.

Indianapolis, Indiana

Indianapolis was one of the few cities where students were bused from the city to the suburbs. Such an action had been outlawed by the 1974 *Milliken* ruling, except in cases in which segregation was intentional. In 1975, an appeals court found a reason to allow interdistrict busing in Indianapolis. In 1969, that city and the suburban Marion County had merged governments but did not merge school systems, prompting the appeals court to conclude that the school systems had been left separate for the benefit of white suburban families. Therefore, a desegregation plan was implemented. Thousands of African American students would be bused to the suburbs (some spending more than an hour a day on the bus), and white students would be bused as well.

When the busing finally began in 1981, the principal of Bunker Hill School found reason to be optimistic. "I stand on the playground and watch the kids," Larry J. Renihan said, "and I see four white kids and two black kids on the swings. Then one of the black kids gets off, and I think, 'Why is he getting off?' Then I see: The black kid got off to push the white kid to get his swing going again."

Despite such heart-warming stories of diversity, the tragic result of the Indianapolis busing program was massive white flight and in-school segregation. Over the next three decades, tens of thousands of white students left the public school system for private, parochial, or charter schools.

Within the integrated schools, white students tended to dominate the upper-tier programs. As the *Washington Post* observed about a suburban school, Broad Ripple, in 1998, "Indianapolis' careful desegregation measures bring a mix of black and white students to Broad Ripple's door every morning, only to resegregate them all over again by the time they sit down for class."

Despite the millions of dollars spent on desegregation and all the accompanying heartache, the Indianapolis desegregation plan was deemed a failure. By the 2000s, the suburban schools were still mostly white and the city schools predominantly black, with black students scoring much lower on standardized tests. White flight was so drastic that from 1971 to 2005 the school district closed approximately one hundred schools.

Detroit, Michigan (revisited)

In Detroit, the attempt at city-to-suburb desegregation was shot down with the *Milliken* ruling. Had it passed, it would have led to upheaval throughout the metropolitan area. There was no way that white suburban parents would have sent their children to schools in Detroit, which many suburbanites were even afraid to drive through.

Black students arrive at Fleming Elementary School on Detroit's east side on January 26, 1976, as the court-ordered busing began.

After the ruling, Detroit School Board president C. L. Golightly did not want to pursue intracity desegregation because the vast majority of public school students were black. Busing to achieve a slightly better racial balance, he thought, would be of little help and little benefit—and, in fact, would prompt more white flight.

Nevertheless, U.S. District Judge Robert E. Masacio ordered the city to desegregate in 1976. Close to 22,000 of Detroit's 247,500 students would be bused. Whites were bused to predominantly black schools, and blacks were bused to schools that had a relatively large white population. Trying to avoid white flight, Masacio did not bus white students to the high-crime, nearly all-black inner-city schools. But busing in itself prompted many whites to leave the school system. By the end of the century, whites comprised only 12 percent of Detroit's population and just 6 percent of the public school composition.

Baton Rouge, Louisiana

Buoyed by the 1954 *Brown* decision, black parents in Baton Rouge sued the school board in 1956 for running a segregated system. *Davis et al. v. East Baton Rouge Parish School Board* would drag on in the courts for forty-seven years.

In 1981, U.S. District Judge John Parker finally took dramatic steps to end the dual school system. Students from black schools would be bused to white schools, and vice versa. The result was predictable. Many white families moved out of the school district, and many of the whites who stayed enrolled their students in private schools—including those that were quickly constructed to satisfy the swelling demand. From 1980 to 2000, the percentage of white private school students in East Baton Rouge jumped from less than twenty to almost fifty.

These two youngsters, too young for school
and too young to know what school integration
really is, were among many carrying signs of
protest as the state legislature met in Baton
Rouge, Louisiana, on November 17, 1960.

John Pierre, an NAACP attorney, was unmoved. "When you consider the attitudes of Baton Rougeans at the time, I would rather they left," Pierre said. "So what, they left. There is no rule that says you have to have whites to have a quality education system."

But you do have to have money, and when whites left Baton Rouge they took their tax-paying dollars with them. By the late 1990s, close to half of the city's black schoolchildren lived in poverty.

In 1996, plaintiffs in the Davis case, including the NAACP, reached an agreement with the school board. Instead of concentrating on busing, they agreed on infusing a large amount of money into the public school system, particularly historically black schools. However, the $2.2 billion proposal was put to a vote of the citizenry, who overwhelmingly voted it down. Stephen J. Caldas and Carl L. Bankston wrote that "members of the middle class had little interest in taxing themselves for a system many had fled."

Norfolk, Virginia

Like many cities and towns across the South, Norfolk had a sordid history of segregation. Lolita Portis-Jones was one of the "Norfolk 17"—African American students who integrated the white schools in 1959. Just twelve years old, Lolita arrived for her first day at Blair Junior High amid a massive police presence. Inside the school, humiliation awaited.

According to the *Virginian Pilot*, "The homeroom teacher gave the white students tissues to put over their faces, as if Portis-Jones had contaminated the room, she said. When she walked into the gym or a class, students started singing the new hit song, 'Charlie Brown,' but with different lyrics: 'Fe-fe, fi-fi, fo-fo, fum, I smell a nigger in the gymnasium.'"

In Norfolk, desegregation was debated for years. In 1972, a federal district court mandated a busing plan that involved the transfer of more than 48,000 students—half black and half white. The order was implemented, and in 1975 a federal judge determined that the desegregation plan had resulted in "unitary" status. This meant that Norfolk no longer had a dual, or segregated, system.

In 1981, Norfolk School Board members—tired of mandatory desegregation—voted to end busing and return to neighborhood schools. They did so because they believed the Reagan administration wouldn't stop them. "I realized that the [Department of Justice] might go along with a plan to end busing," said Norfolk School Board chairman Thomas Johnson. "I wouldn't have done it if I thought I would have to fight the U.S. government."

White students from outlying areas of Norfolk, Virginia, arrive by bus at inner-city Booker T. Washington High School in Norfolk, formerly almost all-black, on September 4, 1970.

93

Johnson's hunch was right. Referring to Norfolk in 1984, the U.S. Justice Department declared that a school board could eliminate a court-ordered busing plan as long as the board was not "motivated by an intent to discriminate." This was a groundbreaking step in the dismantling of school busing.

The Justice Department declared, "Any argument that a school board that has eliminated all effects of past discrimination must nonetheless continue to avoid all policies that increase racial segregation amounts to an assertion that there is a constitutional right to attend racially balanced schools." In the Supreme Court's opinion, the Justice Department said, no such constitutional right existed.

"What the Justice Department has done is outrageous," said Napoleon B. Williams Jr. of the NAACP Legal Defense and Education Fund. "The Justice Department should be protecting constitutional rights. It should not be making political statements."

Norfolk didn't end school busing immediately but instead phased it out slowly. The school board discontinued the busing of elementary school children in 1986 and middle school students in 2001. The busing in high schools continued.

Seattle, Washington

Seattle became the first large city to voluntarily adopt a busing program. In 1978, the school board and other civic leaders decided that Seattle had too many racially imbalanced schools—twenty-six, to be exact. They aimed for diversity through busing and magnet schools, and it wasn't long before 14,000 of the city's 46,000 students were bused out of their neighborhoods, some by choice, mostly to magnet schools.

Although Seattle avoided the Boston-like hysteria, most citizens were not pleased with the new system. That very year, Washington residents voted on Initiative 350, an antibusing proposition. Sixty-six percent of statewide voters, including

61 percent of Seattle residents, voted to end the city's busing program.

The passage of Initiative 350 left many people scratching their heads. Stated the *Washington Post*: "The question is whether Initiative 350 is racially discriminatory. Is it racism to ban busing no court ever ordered? Is the school system run by its locally elected school board or by statewide referenda?"

The case would be decided by the U.S. Supreme Court, but not until 1982. Meanwhile, the buses rolled. Ronald Lynch, a white high school sophomore, rode nine miles to Benjamin Franklin High School in a black working-class area. He eventually transferred to a private school. "I'm not comfortable in this neighborhood," Lynch said. "And besides, the goal of busing is to integrate people of different races so they will know how to cope with each other and deal with each other in the future. Instead, what's happening here is that we brought segregation inside the school. We segregate into our own private groups—blacks, Asians, whites."

While the school board had voted six to one to implement busing, the sole dissenter, Ellen Roe, made a strong accusation. Roe, a white mother of six children, claimed that the busing plan was aimed to appease whites who lived in the city. According to Roe, they didn't like that their children were outnumbered by black kids in the classroom. Through busing, white kids would be bused to the city schools, where they would provide more same-race friends for their children. "They used the black people," Roe said. "It didn't have anything to do with a great burning desire for integration."

On June 30, 1982, the Supreme Court handed down its decision on Initiative 350. The court ruled that it was unconstitutional. It stated, "The initiative removes the authority [school board] to address a racial problem [racially imbalanced schools]," resulting in "a burden [to] minority interests." The Seattle busing plan continued for almost the rest of the century, finally ending in 1999.

Los Angeles, California

From 1978 to 1981, Los Angeles families rode a "roller coaster of mandatory busing," according to L.A. School Board president Roberta Weintraub. A busing plan in Los Angeles was implemented during the Carter administration and then abandoned just three months after Ronald Reagan took office.

L.A. schools were a mix of white, black, and Hispanic students, but some schools were deemed too white. For the 1978-79 school year, Los Angeles Superior Court Judge Paul Egly ordered mandatory busing for 23,000 of the school district's 529,000 students.

Most Californians objected to the plan, and they did so with their votes. In fact, Republican Bobbi Fiedler scored an upset in her 1980 run for Congress because she opposed busing and her Democratic opponent was for it. "What busing does is drive out the middle class—white, black and brown," Fiedler said. "People feel it's racist in itself and that it denies freedom. Parents who can afford a change simply will not put up with having their children bused from a higher achieving school to a lower achieving school."

California voters voiced their displeasure in 1979 with their support of Proposition 1. By a two to one margin, they voted to prohibit court-ordered busing unless it was intended to correct intentional segregation. In December 1980, the Court of Appeals for the Second District in Los Angeles stated that segregation in L.A. was not intentional—that it was instead caused by housing patterns. The California Supreme Court let stand the appeals court's decision.

NAACP attorneys tried to get the U.S. Supreme Court to hear the case, but the court refused the request. In April 1981, mandatory busing ended in California. All 23,000 affected students were allowed to return to their neighborhood schools. Julio Valazquez, an eighth-grader who had been bused to a faraway school, said he was "just happy to be near home again."

"I doubt whether these decisions were being made in the best interest of the youngsters," said Pacoima Junior High School principal William Zazueta. "I think the busing program was primarily the movement of minority youngsters, to their detriment. Society must look for methods to improve integration, but I wish society would stop using the public schools to solve its problems."

St. Louis, Missouri

In 1975, Judge James Meredith ruled that St. Louis schools were segregated. However, in order to avoid further white flight—most of the city's public school kids were already predominantly black—Meredith pushed for the creation of magnet schools and the hiring of more minority teachers. At a 1979 trial, Meredith ruled that St. Louis schools were *unintentionally* segregated, due to housing patterns.

In 1980, a federal appeals court ruled differently. It stated that St. Louis schools had been intentionally segregated in the first half of the twentieth century and that the school board had failed to take necessary steps to rectify the situation. The case went back to Judge Meredith, who ordered a desegregation plan. But there was just one problem. Only 23 percent of St. Louis public school students were white, and they were concentrated in certain neighborhoods.

By 1983, the city and sixteen suburban districts agreed on an intercity busing plan. White suburban families would not have to fret about sending their kids to the city. Instead, 12,000 black students would be bused to suburban schools. Since this number was relatively small (the St. Louis metro area population in 1980 was 2.4 million), white schools were not "deluged" with black students.

The busing plan continued through 1999, but overall it didn't change the educations of or help African American students. Statistics from the 2004 Missouri Assessment Program revealed little improvement in academic achievement.

Students board buses at Shaw Visual and Performing Arts Elementary School, a magnet school in the St. Louis public school system. A quota system designed to help integrate St. Louis public schools is keeping thousands of students from open spots at sought-after magnet schools.

New York, New York

In New York City in 1970, about half of the public schools were either 90-plus percent black or 90-plus percent white. For years, residents wondered if a federal court would mandate a desegregation plan, but it never happened.

New York's boroughs—Brooklyn, Manhattan, Queens, Bronx, and Staten Island—implemented limited amounts of busing and school rezoning, but were afraid to push the issue too hard. Desegregation was expensive, white flight was inevitable, and opposition to desegregation was fierce. Moreover, "busing" to faraway schools in New York City was impractical, since traffic was exceptionally heavy and most kids walked to school.

In some cases, a school board or a judge ordered the desegregation of a particular school, which usually created conflict. One Jewish couple complained about the treatment of their son after he was assigned to a predominantly African American school. "Each school year," they stated, "he received certificates for his achievement. . . . This year, after attending school for two days in the sixth grade, he refused to go any longer. For participating actively in class, he has been called 'Jewish faggot' and shot at with paper clips from catapults by his black classmates, because he 'knows everything.'"

The most dramatic event occurred in the Rosedale neighborhood of Queens. Rosedale Junior High kids attended Intermediate School (I.S.) 231. Because the school was predominantly black and overcrowded, many white families pulled their children out of the school. But in 1978, white families celebrated a decision by the Queens School Board. To alleviate overcrowding at I.S. 231 and to curtail white flight from Rosedale, the school board established an I.S. 231 annex school in the white area of Rosedale.

White children filled up the annex school, leaving the
main I.S. 231 with an even higher percentage of black students. This prompted the ire of the Federal Office of Civil
Rights. Threatened by the loss of federal funding, New York
City Public School chancellor Frank Macchiarola ordered the
transfer of 450 seventh- and eighth-graders from the annex
school to the main school.

Parents of the annex students were outraged. Sheila
Pecoraro had sent her three older children to the main school,
but she refused to let her youngest go back there. "[My] other
children never knew what it was like to go to the bathroom,"
she said. "Any child at 231 knew never to go to the bathroom
because they'd be beaten up and mugged."

African American Barbara Weisenfeld, a leader of the
parents' association at the main school, resented what she
considered inflammatory accusations. "The white parents
magnify incidents here," she said. "They intended to create
problems so they would have a leg to stand on. They operate
from a position of fear."

Nevertheless, white parents were so passionate about the
issue that in February 1981 they staged a sit-in inside the annex.
Police evicted protesters and arrested those who wouldn't
leave. It wasn't long before the annex was officially closed.

Students head for buses after the first day of school at Abesgami High School in Galloway Township, New Jersey.

chapter 7

The Return to Segregation

While some cities still bus students to achieve racial balance, most busing programs have been terminated. A large number of American schools are still segregated. According to a 2009 report by The Civil Rights Project, about two-thirds of black and Latino students in large cities attend schools with less than 10 percent white students. About one in six black students goes to a school that is at least 99 percent minority.

"It's getting to the point of almost absolute segregation in the worst of the segregated cities—within one or two percentage points of what the Old South used to be like," said Gary Orfield, codirector of The Civil Rights Project. "The biggest metro areas are the epicenters of segregation. It's getting worse for both blacks and Latinos, and nothing is being done about it."

The move away from busing developed steadily during the last decade of the twentieth century. The 1991 Supreme Court ruling in *Board of Education of Oklahoma City v. Dowell* outlined how courts could release school districts from their obligations to maintain desegregated schools. After the ruling, a district that showed it had been taking the proper steps to desegregate could be declared "unitary" (no longer segregated) and was thus freed from court oversight. In *Freeman v. Pitts* in 1992, the Supreme Court ruled that schools could fulfill their obligations in an incremental fashion—a decision that made it easier to achieve unitary status.

Clint Bolick, of the conservative-leaning Institute for Justice, rejoiced, saying the ruling marked "the beginning of the end for the regime of forced busing that has destroyed school systems and communities around the nation."

Theoretically, a district deemed unitary could be put under court control again if, for example, a plaintiff won a lawsuit that claimed segregation. But in practice, there was a remote chance of that happening.

By the mid-1990s, school districts in such cities as Savannah, Georgia, and Oklahoma City were declared unitary. In 1995, Denver and Wilmington were freed from their busing obligations. Other antibusing campaigns were waged that year. Governor Fife Symington launched a campaign to release all of Arizona's school districts from federal court orders. In Indianapolis, the school board took steps to end fourteen years of busing in that city. The trend would continue throughout the country.

Not everyone was happy to see busing end. In a 1990 Harris poll, 50 percent of those earning less than $15,000 a year said they favored busing to achieve racial balance. And in a 1987 poll by Harris, three-quarters of parents whose children were bused were "very satisfied" with busing. Apparently, while the horror stories of busing still existed, busing was quietly succeeding in many communities. "Ask the people who've had busing, and you'll see," Harris claimed. "Busing generally works."

Said Patricia Tweedle, the assistant principal at Beasley Elementary School in Chicago, in 1995, "Busing is a curriculum in itself because you're enhancing integration; you're enhancing the cultural experiences of the child when they all share their cultures. The busing program works fine for us. We need our busing, we depend on our busing."

Not everyone agreed. Busing seemed especially futile in those big cities in which school populations were becoming overwhelmingly black and Latino. Spending millions of dollars to bus students so that they could sit next to a handful of white kids seemed pointless. In such cities, many argued, segregation wasn't the real problem; bad, underfunded schools were the real issue. Said U.S. congressman Martin Hoke, "You could argue in the Cleveland public school system, everybody has the same education, and it's utterly substandard."

On July 14, 1999, Boston reached a historic milestone when the school board decided to drop race as a factor in determining where students would go to school. The school board made the decision while under the pall of a federal lawsuit, which claimed that the system discriminated against white children. Since 1989, Boston had used a "controlled choice" plan for elementary and middle school students that was intended to appease all sides. Under the system, a school reserved some of its space for students outside the neighborhood—a plan that locked out some students from their neighborhood schools.

In Boston, busing clearly hadn't worked. The white student population plummeted from 60 percent in the early 1970s to 15 percent in 1999. The reason was threefold: Boston, like the rest of the nation, had trended toward suburbanization; Latino and Asian immigration had greatly increased in Boston, as it had

throughout the country; and busing had exacerbated Boston's white flight. Considering that six out of seven Boston students were nonwhite, "there is nothing for busing to do," said Harvard University sociology professor Orlando Patterson.

Yet even in Boston, all was not hopeless. In 2006, the city won the Broad Prize for Urban Education as the most improved big-city school district in the country. Much of the credit went to Thomas W. Payzant, the superintendent of Boston Public Schools from 1995 to 2006. Payzant divided high schools into smaller schools so that students could get more individualized attention. He also spent a tremendous amount of time with students, learning about their needs and concerns while also imparting words of wisdom.

Mayor Thomas Menino and school superintendent Thomas Payzant, right, at a news conference in Boston in July 1999.

"How many of you have started to think about college?" Payzant asked a class at Hyde Park High School in 2005.

"I don't want to go," replied a sophomore boy, who said he wanted to manage a McDonald's. "It's a waste of time. I already know my stuff."

"A high school diploma is not going to be enough, my friend," Payzant says. "Don't tell me you're not smart. Start thinking college now."

Payzant thought that dedication, communication, and smart decisions on the part of the educators were the keys to improved schools, at least in Boston. From 1998 to 2008, the percentage of Boston students who passed the state exams in mathematics rose from 23 to 84. The percentage of those who passed in reading soared from 43 to 91.

In recent decades, many school systems have turned to magnet schools as an alternative to busing. Many magnet schools are strong in a certain discipline, such as science or the arts, and thus attract students who are geared toward those subjects. In most cases, students have to test into a magnet school or be chosen in a lottery. Racial quotas have long been a factor in the admissions process. Magnet schools tend to attract motivated teachers and are usually significantly better than a city's regular public schools.

Magnet schools have provided students from different neighborhoods and races the opportunity to attend a good school with a diverse student body. But this system also can be seen as exclusionary. What about the qualified students who can't get in because of racial quotas or the luck of the lottery? Moreover, many highly acclaimed magnet high schools are largely white because, in part, white students had the benefit of better elementary and middle schools and thus scored better on entrance exams. Also, since magnet schools attract the best teachers and students, the remaining public schools are left with less experienced or qualified teachers.

Some critics claim that magnet schools exist to appease middle-class urban white families. White families will stay in the city and send their kids to a public school, the critics allege, but only if it's a magnet school. Said African American Elridge McMillan, president of the Southern Education Foundation in Atlanta, "[I]f you're going to have magnet schools, put some of the good magnet schools in our sections of town."

Beginning in the early 1990s, charter schools emerged across the country as an alternative to conventional public schools. A charter school is funded by public dollars, but it is overseen by a board of parents or community members, a government agency, a nonprofit organization, a university, or a corporation. Charter schools, which don't charge tuition, typically have fewer regulations and restrictions than public schools. This allows educators to employ innovative techniques. These schools often specialize in one or two subject areas, such as science, and their class sizes are typically smaller. Many charter schools require children to wear uniforms and have longer school days.

Because so many public school systems have poor reputations, charter schools have mushroomed at a phenomenal rate. Today, more than 5,000 charter schools operate in the United States, educating more than 1.5 million children. Critics of charter schools say that they disrupt the public school system and could eventually lead to the privatization of public schools. They also say that there's no conclusive evidence that charter schools produce more successful students. Even Geoffrey Canada, chief executive officer of the Harlem Children's Zone and its renowned charter school program, admits that there "are many examples of good charter public schools that should be replicated, and there are lousy ones that should be closed."

Some charter schools have produced dramatic results. In 2010, the New York City Department of Education reported that charter school eighth-graders outscored the city's public school eighth-graders by nearly 18 percentage points in science.

The leaders of the Harlem Children's Zone, which serves more than 10,000 children in a predominantly African American section of New York City, aims to educate and support each child from his and her earliest years up until college. Their innovative efforts include The Baby College parenting workshops, the Harlem Gems preschool program, the Promise Academy, a high-quality public charter school, and an obesity program to help children stay healthy. Students are fed healthy meals and participate in daily physical activity. At Promise Academy II, 100 percent of the third-graders were at or above grade level on the 2008 statewide math test.

"This [The Harlem Children's Zone] is quite literally about saving young lives," Canada said. "For parents in devastated neighborhoods such as Harlem, the decision to send their child to the local failure factory or a successful charter school is no choice."

"Failure factory" may seem like harsh language, but it is a term used frequently to describe urban public schools. In 2005, only 38 percent of Cleveland public school students graduated in four years. Compare that to Loyola Academy in the wealthy suburb of Wilmette, Illinois, where 99 percent not only graduate each year but go on to four-year colleges or universities. Claimed the Civil Rights Project report, authored by Gary Orfield, "Millions of nonwhite students are locked into 'dropout factory' high schools, where huge percentages do not graduate, have little future in the American economy, and almost none are well prepared for college."

Orfield asserted that even a bright, determined student has a hard time succeeding in such a school: "Many are in high schools where there is no real path to college because there

The Harlem Children's Zone

are not enough teachers credentialed and experienced in key subjects and not enough fellow students ready to enroll in strong pre-collegiate courses taught at an appropriate level. For those students, there is no way to get the right preparation in their school regardless of their personal talent and motivation."

In 2010, the U.S. Department of Education announced that twenty-one cities would receive planning grants for Promise Neighborhoods, named after Harlem's Promise Academy. With the one-year grants, the recipients would create plans to provide cradle-to-career services that would improve the educational achievement and healthy development of children. For his 2012 budget, President Obama proposed $150 million to support the implementation of Promise Neighborhood projects.

Perhaps The Harlem Children's Zone is a better model for improving the education offered to students in poorer neighborhoods. Hopefully, this won't lead to the racially charged conflicts that erupted around court-ordered busing.

TIMELINE

May 17, 1954: In *Brown v. Board of Education*, the U.S. Supreme Court declares segregation in public schools unconstitutional.

May 31, 1955: In *Brown II*, the Supreme Court establishes guidelines for undoing segregated public education, although it does not establish a timetable.

September 24, 1957: President Eisenhower orders the federal guard to help nine African American students integrate Central High School in Little Rock, Arkansas. It is one of many school integration battles in the South in the years after the *Brown* decision.

1961–62: The NAACP challenges segregated schools in fifty-five school districts in the Midwest, West, and Northeast.

July 2, 1964: President Lyndon Johnson signs the Civil Rights Act of 1964. It authorizes the Department of Health, Education, and Welfare to withhold funds to any district that excludes students from schools on the basis of race. It also authorizes the attorney general to initiate class-action lawsuits against schools that do not conform to the law.

1966: The federally commissioned "Coleman Report" finds that black students in racially mixed classrooms perform better than those in all-black schools.

May 27, 1968: In *Green v. School Board of New Kent County*, the U.S. Supreme Court demands that public schools desegregate as soon as possible.

October 29, 1969: In *Alexander v. Holmes County Board of Education*, the U.S. Supreme Court demands that thirty-three Mississippi school districts desegregate immediately.

1969 to 1974: During his time in office, antibusing president Richard Nixon appoints three Supreme Court justices and a chief justice.

April 20, 1971: In *Swann v. Charlotte-Mecklenburg Board of Education*, the U.S. Supreme Court declares that segregation is unconstitutional even if it is caused by geographic proximity rather than by an intent to segregate.

1972: The number of black students attending minority schools (90 percent or more minority) in the South has dropped from 78 percent to 25 percent since 1968.

June 21, 1973: The U.S. Supreme Court ruling in *Keyes v. School District No. 1* helps open up school systems across the United States to legal desegregation action.

June 21, 1974: U.S. District Court Judge W. Arthur Garrity Jr. issues a desegregation plan, based on the massive busing of students, for Boston's public schools.

July 25, 1974: In *Milliken v. Bradley*, the U.S. Supreme Court puts limitations on interdistrict school busing.

September 12, 1974: The first day of court-ordered busing in Boston is marked by protests and violence.

September 16, 1974: Some three hundred antibusing rioters damage public property and assault black citizens in Boston.

October 4, 1974: Thousands of antibusers march on "National Boycott Day."

September 1975: Phase II of Judge Garrity's desegregation plan in Boston begins; an extra 7,000 students must be bused. ROAR responds with a protest march through the Charlestown neighborhood.

September 4–5, 1975: Two hundred people are arrested in Louisville, Kentucky, during antibusing rioting.

1981: The Reagan administration successfully pushes Congress to rescind the Emergency School Aid Act of 1982, which had provided federal funds to state and local governments that were forced to desegregate.

1981: A CBS/*New York Times* poll finds that 77 percent of Americans oppose busing and only 17 percent favor it.

1981 to 1993: In their twelve years in office, Presidents Reagan and George H. W. Bush appoint six justices to the U.S. Supreme Court, leading to conservative decisions in school desegregation cases.

1984: Since 1974, the number of white public school students in Boston has dropped from 53,593 to 15,257.

January 15, 1991: In *Board of Education of Oklahoma City v. Dowell*, the U.S. Supreme Court outlines how courts can release school districts from their obligations to maintain desegregated schools.

March 31, 1992: In *Freeman v. Pitts* in 1992, the U.S. Supreme Court rules that schools can fulfill their obligations in an incremental fashion—a decision that makes it easier to achieve unitary status.

Early 1990s: Publicly financed charter schools emerge across the country as an alternative to conventional public schools.

1995: It is reported that only 38 percent of Cleveland's public school students in the previous school year graduated in four years.

July 14, 1999: The Boston school board decides to drop race as a factor in determining where students will go to school.

2009: The Civil Rights Project reports that about one in six black students goes to a school that is at least 99 percent minority—evidence of the resegregation of America's public schools.

SOURCES

CHAPTER 1: The "Master Plan"

p. 10,   "Epithets flew . . ." Louis P. Masur, "The Photograph That Shocked America, and the Victim Who Stepped Outside the Frame," March 2008, http://digitaljournalist.org/issue0803/the-photograph-that-shocked-america-and-the-victim-who-stepped-outside-the-frame.html.

p. 10,   "get the nigger," Ibid.

p. 12,   "When the kids . . ." "Boston Under the Phase I Plan," Watson.org, 1998, http://www.watson.org/~lisa/blackhistory/school-integration/boston/phase1.html.

p. 12,   "Every day when . . ." "Busing's Boston Massacre," www.tri-county.tc/files/uploads/pdf-files/Assignments/boston-busing.pdf.

p. 12,   "the most unpopular . . ." Lawrence Feinberg, "Busing Orders Said To Widen Isolation," *Washington Post*, May 15, 1981.

p. 13,   "I've looked at . . ." B. Drummond Ayres Jr., "Civil Rights Groups Fear a Slowdown in Busing for Desegregation of Schools," *New York Times*, December 21, 1980.

p. 13,   "That's simply not . . ." Ibid.

CHAPTER 2: How Busing Began

p. 17,   "lacked furniture and . . ." Catherine Reef, *Education and Learning in America* (New York: Infobase Publishing, 2009), 159.

p. 17,   "how we walked . . ." Betty Collier-Thomas, *Jesus, Jobs, and Justice: African American Women and Religion* (New York: Alfred A. Knopf, 2010), 438.

p. 18,   "I want to . . ." Raymond Arsenault, *The Wild Ass of the Ozarks* (Philadelphia: Temple University Press, 1984), 205-206.

p. 19,   "No State shall . . ." "14th Amendment," Cornell Law University, http://topics.law.cornell.edu/constitution/amendmentxiv.

p. 20,   "the judicious placement . . ." Charles T. Clotfelter, *After Brown: The Rise and Retreat of School Desegregation* (Princeton, N.J.: Princeton University Press, 2004), 20.

p. 23,   "secure justice," Clayborne Carson, *Civil Rights Chronicle* (Lincolnwood, Ill.: Legacy Publishing, 2003), 115.

p. 23,   "[e]qual means getting . . ." Ibid., 123.

p. 24,   "We conclude, unanimously . . ." Ibid., 121.

pp 24-25,   "enter such orders . . ." "Brown v. Board of Education," http://www.nationalcenter.org/cc0725.htm.

p. 25,   "Human blood may . . ." Editorial, *Jackson Daily News*, May 18, 1954.

p. 25,   "their sweet little . . ." Garth E. Pauley, *The Modern Presidency & Civil Rights: Rhetoric on Race from Roosevelt to Nixon* (College Station: Texas A&M University Press, 2001), 62.

p. 28,   "They've gone in . . ." Carson, *Civil Rights Chronicle*, 156.

CHAPTER 3: Rev Up the Buses

p. 33,   "Coleman, more than . . ." Barbara J. Kiviat, "The Social Side of Schooling," *Johns Hopkins Magazine*, April 2000, http://www.jhu.edu/jhumag/0400web/18.html.

p. 34,   "the state, acting . . ." "Charles C. Green et al. v. County School Board
          of New Kent County, Virginia," Encyclopedia Virginia, http://www.
          encyclopediavirginia.org/Green_Charles_C_et_al_v_County_School_
          Board_of_New_Kent_County_Virginia.

p. 34,   "affirmative duty to . . ." Robert Hamlett Bremner, *Children in America: A
          Documentary History, Volumes 1-3* (Cambridge, Mass.: Harvard University
          Press, 1974), 1840.

p. 34,   "The burden on . . ." Ibid., 1841.

p. 34,   "When this opinion . . ." "Charles C. Green et al. v. County School Board of
          New Kent County, Virginia."

p. 34,   "each of the . . ." Kern Alexander and M. David Alexander, *American Public
          School Law* (Florence, Ky.: Cengage Learning, 2005), 905.

pp. 35-36, "the first remedial . . ." "Swann v. Charlotte-Mecklenburg Board of
          Education," Cornell University Law School, http://www.law.cornell.edu/
          supct/html/historics/USSC_CR_0402_0001_ZS.html.

p. 36,   "local authorities and . . ." Ibid.

p. 40,   "in this district . . ." Stephen J. Caldas and Carl L. Bankston, *Forced to Fail:
          The Paradox of School Desegregation* (Lanham, Md.: Rowman & Littlefield
          Education, 2007), 148.

p. 40,   "Schools are no . . ." Tom Wicker, "Busing After a Decade," *New York Times*,
          June 26, 1981.

p. 40,   "I lived in . . ." Kendra R. Johnson, "African-American Richmond:
          Educational Segregation and Desegregation," Virginia Black History
          Archives, http://www.library.vcu.edu/jbc/speccoll/vbha/school/turnage.html.

p. 41,   "only remedy promising . . ." "School Busing," The Civil Rights Movement
          in Virginia, http://www.vahistorical.org/civilrights/busing.htm.

p. 42,   "Teachers started placing . . ." Kendra R. Johnson, "African-American
          Richmond: Educational Segregation and Desegregation."

p. 42,   "Busing to create . . ." Richard A. Pride, *The Burden of Busing: The
          Politics of Desegregation in Nashville, Tennessee* (Knoxville: University of
          Tennessee Press, 1995), 71.

p. 43,   "We don't have . . ." Ibid., 72.

p. 44,   "When I was . . ." Caldas and Bankston, *Forced to Fail*, 173.

p. 44,   "It was not . . ." Ibid.

p. 44,   "the black parents . . ." Kevin Uhrich, "Leaving No Child Behind," *Pasadena
          Weekly*, April 5, 2007, http://www.pasadenaweekly.com/cms/story/
          detail/?IssueNum=66&id=4509.

p. 44,   "by use of . . ." Caldas and Bankston, *Forced to Fail*, 33.

p. 45,   "The Keyes case . . ." Ibid.

p. 45,   "within the definition . . ." Beverly Daniel Tatum, *Can We Talk about Race?
          And Other Conversations in an Era of School Resegregation* (Boston: Beacon
          Press: 2007), 9.

p. 46,   "no showing of . . ." "Milliken v. Bradley," Courtroom View Network, http://
          lawschool.courtroomview.com/acf_cases/9667-milliken-v-bradley.

p. 47,   "Michigan, by one . . ." "Milliken v. Bradley," Cornell University Law School, http://www.law.cornell.edu/supct/html/historics/USSC_CR_0418_0717_ZD.html.

p. 47,   "[U]nless our children . . ." Jeanne H. Ballantine and Joan Z. Spade, *Schools and Society: A Sociological Approach to Education* (Thousand Oaks, Cal.: Pine Forge Press, 2007), 345.

CHAPTER 4: The Fury in Boston

p. 49,   "Get those niggers . . ." Saul Wisnia, *Fenway Park: The Centennial* (New York: St. Martin's Press, 2011), 71.

p. 50,   "should stay with . . ." Thomas H. O'Connor, *South Boston: My Home Town* (Boston: Northeastern University Press, 1994), 209.

p. 50,   "and other residents . . ." Ibid.

p. 51,   "knowingly carried out . . ." Kenneth T. Jackson, Karen Markoe, and Arnie Markoe, *The Scribner Encyclopedia of American Lives, Volume 5* (New York: Simon & Schuster, 2001), 217.

p. 51,   "drew a series . . ." O'Connor, *South Boston*, 216.

p. 53,   "You're a disgrace . . ." Ronald P. Formisano, *Boston Against Busing: Race, Class, and Ethnicity in the 1960s and 1970s* (Chapel Hill: The University of North Carolina Press, 2004), 76.

p. 53,   "It was great . . ." Ibid., 77.

p. 54,   "Well, when we . . ." Henry Hampton and Steve Fayer, *Voices of Freedom: An Oral History of the Civil Rights Movement from the 1950s Through the 1980s* (New York: Bantam Books, 1990), 600-601.

p. 54,   "What I saw . . ." Ibid, 601.

p. 55,   "I said, Why . . ." Ibid., 606.

p. 55,   "I want my . . ." Stephan Thernstrom and Abigail Thernstrom, *America in Black and White: One Nation Indivisible* (New York: Simon & Schuster, 1999), 331.

p. 57,   "I have consistently . . ." Marshall Cavendish Corporation, *America in the 20th Century, 1970-1979* (Tarrytown, N.Y.: Marshall Cavendish, 2003), 1075.

p. 57,   "Sometimes when I . . ." Neal P. McCluskey, *Feds in the Classroom: How Big Government Corrupts, Cripples, and Compromises American Education* (Lanham, Md.: Rowman & Littlefield, 2007), 48.

p. 59,   "deliberate policy of . . ." "Education: More Trouble on The Busing Route," *Time*, September 1, 1975, http://www.time.com/time/magazine/article/0,9171,947171,00.html.

p. 59,   "Eighty percent of . . ." Carson, *Civil Rights Chronicle*, 387.

p. 59,   "They shall not . . ." Jean Strouse, *Newsweek*, May 5, 1975.

p. 59,   "We're frightened . . ." Peter Goldman, "The Roar of ROAR," *Newsweek*, June 9, 1975.

p. 61,   "We are asking . . ." Jean Strouse, "Mean Streets of Boston," *Newsweek*, September 22, 1975.

p. 61,   "That's right . . ." Ibid.

p. 61,   "The parents are . . ." Ibid.

p. 61,   "These people feel . . ." Ibid.

pp. 61-62,   "If you're going . . ." Ibid.

p. 62,   "I'd go into . . ." Ibid.

p. 63,   "The racial balance . . ." Gene I. Maeroff, "Boston's Decade of Desegregation Leaves Experts Disputing Effects," *New York Times*, December 28, 1984.

p. 63,   "The sustained guerrilla . . ." James N. Baker and Eileen Keerdoja, "A Truce in Southie," *Newsweek*, November 27, 1978.

p. 64,   "The desegregation order . . ." Gene I. Maeroff, "Boston's Decade of Desegregation Leaves Experts Disputing Effects."

p. 64,   "A lot of . . ." Ibid.

p. 64,   "took away the . . ." "Busing's Boston Massacre," Hoover Institution, Stanford University, http://www.hoover.org/publications/policy-review/article/7768.

p. 64,   "When schools were . . ." Matthew Connelly and Paul Kennedy, "Must It Be the Rest Against the West?" Hudson, Florida, http://www.hudsonfla.com/west.htm.

p. 65,   "had a paternalistic . . ." Ibid.

p. 65,   "I'll miss it . . ." Ibid.

CHAPTER 5: Battles on Capitol Hill

p. 67,   "Vietnam of the . . ." Kenneth J. Heineman, *God Is a Conservative: Religion, Politics, and Morality in Contemporary America* (New York: NYU Press, 1998), 68.

p. 67,   "Suppose a candidate . . ." "Busing to Achieve Desegregation," Novelguide.com, http://www.novelguide.com/a/discover/adec_0001_0008_0/adec_0001_0008_0_02629.html.

pp. 68-69,   "Examining the concepts . . ." "Should School Busing Be Stopped?" *U.S. News & World Report*, September 30, 1974.

pp. 69-70,   "I firmly believe . . ." Ibid.

p. 70,   "believes that his . . ." " 'Statute of Limitations' for School Busing?" *U.S. News & World Report*, June 28, 1976.

p. 70,   "As President, I . . ." Daniel Chu, "Changing Course," *Newsweek*, June 14, 1976.

p. 72,   "Give us three . . ." "'Statue of Limitations' for School Busing?" *U.S. News & World Report*, June 28, 1976.

p. 72,   "to cease judicial . . ." Ibid.

p. 72,   "We have come . . ." Ibid.

p. 76,   "[S]ome of those . . ." Carson, *Civil Rights Chronicle*, 406.

p. 76,   "[C]ompulsory busing of . . ." Gary Orfield and Susan E. Eaton, *Dismantling Desegregation* (New York: The New Press, 1996), 17.

p. 76,   "During this period . . ." Ibid., 17-18.

CHAPTER 6: The Buses Keep Rolling

p. 80,   "I was upset . . ." Seth Davis, *When March Went Mad: The Game That Transformed Basketball* (New York: Macmillan, 2009), 20.

p. 80,   "was very controversial . . ." Ibid.

p. 80,   "Give it up . . ." Earvin "Magic" Johnson and Richard Levin, *Magic* (New York: Signet, 1991), 47.

p. 81,   "I thought everybody . . ." Marcus Wohlsen, "The first day of busing was lonely day in class," September 4, 2005, courier-journal.com, http://www.courier-journal.com/article/20050904/NEWS01/509040418/The-first-day-of-busing-was-lonely-day-in-class.

p. 82,   "I think I'll . . ." "Busing and Strikes: Schools in Turmoil," *Time*, September 15, 1975, http://www.time.com/time/magazine/article/0,9171,917825-1,00.html.

p. 82,   "Communists . . . pigs . . ." Ibid.

p. 83,   "We don't want . . ." Ibid.

p. 83,   "Discipline problems have . . ." Caldas and Bankston, *Forced to Fail*, 151.

p. 85,   "People are scared . . ." Bill Peterson, "Issue of Busing Losing Its Sting Across Country," *Washington Post*, September 4, 1977.

p. 85,   "White parents don't . . ." Sandra Dawson, "Desegregation without Despair," *Black Enterprise*, September 1978.

p. 86,   "It's almost impossible . . ." Bill Peterson, "Issue of Busing Losing Its Sting Across Country."

p. 86,   "It was felt . . ." Sandra Dawson, "Desegregation without Despair."

pp. 86-87,   "Within 30 days . . ." Caldas and Bankston, *Forced to Fail*, 140.

p. 87,   "Go Home Feds . . ." Geoff Winningham, "Football, Game of Life," *Texas Monthly*, October 1983, 75.

p. 88,   "I stand on . . ." Susan Barker, "The 20 Biggest News Stories," *Indianapolis Monthly*, September 1997, 149.

p. 88,   "Indianapolis' careful desegregation . . ." Caldas and Bankston, *Forced to Fail*, 156.

p. 92,   "When you consider . . ." "47-year-old Baton Rouge School Desegregation Case Finally Closes," *Jet*, September 8, 2003, http://findarticles.com/p/articles/mi_m1355/is_11_104/ai_107837336/.

p. 92,   "members of the . . ." Caldas and Bankston, *Forced to Fail*, 145.

p. 92,   "The homeroom teacher . . ." Denise Watson Batts, "The Norfolk 17 Face a Hostile Reception as Schools Reopen," PilotOnline.com, http://hamptonroads.com/2008/09/massive-resistance-17-face-hostile-reception-schools-reopen.

p. 93,   "I realized that . . ." Orfield and Eaton, *Dismantling Desegregation*, 118.

p. 94,   "motivated by an . . ." Leslie Maitland Werner, "U.S. Says Cities Can Put an End to Busing Plans," *New York Times*, December 7, 1984.

p. 94,   "Any argument that . . ." Ibid.

p. 94,   "What the Justice . . ." Ibid.

p. 95,   "The question is . . ." Fred Barbash, "Balancing Act," *Washington Post*, March 22, 1982.

p. 95,   "I'm not comfortable . . ." Ibid.

p. 95,   "They used the . . ." Ibid.

p. 95,　　"The initiative removes . . ." "Supreme Court Report," *ABA Journal: Volume 68*, September 1982, 1155.

p. 96,　　"roller coaster of . . ." Jay Mathews, "Los Angeles Ends Forced Busing," *Washington Post*, April 20, 1981.

p. 96,　　"What busing does . . ." B. Drummond Ayres Jr., "Civil Rights Groups Fear a Slowdown in Busing for Desegregation of Schools," *New York Times*, December 21, 1980.

p. 96,　　"just happy to . . ." Jay Mathews, "Los Angeles Ends Forced Busing."

p. 97,　　"I doubt whether . . ." Ibid.

p. 100,　　"Each school year . . ." Caldas and Bankston, *Forced to Fail*, 174.

p. 101,　　"[My] other children . . ." Serge Schemann, "White View of Queens School Clash . . . ," *New York Times*, February 17, 1981.

p. 101,　　"The white parents . . ." David Bird, "Queens Parents Conduct Classes at Closed School," *New York Times*, February 3, 1981.

CHAPTER 7: The Return to Segregation

p. 103,　　"It's getting to . . ." Amanda Paulson, "Resegregation of U.S. Schools Deepening," *The Christian Science Monitor*, January 25, 2008, http://www.csmonitor.com/USA/Society/2008/0125/p01s01-ussc.html.

p. 104,　　"the beginning of . . ." David Whitman, "Busing's Unheralded Legacy."

p. 105,　　"Ask the people . . ." David Whitman, "Busing's unheralded legacy," *U.S. News & World Report*, April 13, 1992.

p. 105,　　"Busing is a . . ." James L. Tyson, "Chicago Considers Applying Brakes To School Busing," *Christian Science Monitor*, October 19, 1995.

p. 105,　　"You could argue . . ." Peter Applebome, "A Wave of Suits Seeks a Reversal of School Busing," *New York Times*, September 26, 1995.

p. 106,　　"there is nothing . . ." Formisano, *Boston Against Busing*, 252.

p. 107,　　"How many of . . ." Tracy Jan, "Payzant Races to Finish," *Boston Globe*, November 1, 2005.

p. 108,　　"[I]f you're going . . ." Stephen Koff, "Has Busing Outlived Its Usefulness?" *St. Petersburg Times*, January 31, 1991.

p. 108,　　"are many examples . . ." Geoffrey Canada, "The Push-Back on Charter Schools," *New York Times*, March 14, 2010, http://roomfordebate.blogs.nytimes.com/2010/03/14/the-push-back-on-charter-schools/.

p. 109,　　"This [The Harlem Children's Zone] is quite . . ." Ibid.

p. 109,　　"Millions of nonwhite . . ." Gary Orfield, "Reviving the Goal of an Integrated Society," The Civil Rights Project, January 2009, 3.

pp. 109-111, "Many are in . . ." Ibid., 4.

BIBLIOGRAPHY

Alexander, Kern, and M. David Alexander. *American Public School Law*. Florence, Ky.: Cengage Learning, 2005.

Applebome, Peter. "A Wave of Suits Seeks a Reversal of School Busing." *New York Times*, September 26, 1995.

Arsenault, Raymond. *The Wild Ass of the Ozarks*. Philadelphia: Temple University Press, 1984.

Ayers, B. Drummond, Jr. "Civil Rights Groups Fear a Slowdown in Busing for Desegregation of Schools." *New York Times*, December 21, 1980.

Baker, James N., and Eileen Keerdoja. "A Truce in Southie." *Newsweek*, November 27, 1978.

Ballantine, Jeanne H., and Joan Z. Spade. *Schools and Society: A Sociological Approach to Education*. Thousand Oaks, Cal.: Pine Forge Press, 2007.

Barbash, Fred. "Balancing Act." *Washington Post*, March 22, 1982.

Barker, Susan. "The 20 Biggest News Stories." *Indianapolis Monthly*, September 1997.

Batts, Denise Watson. "The Norfolk 17 Face a Hostile Reception as Schools Reopen." PilotOnline.com, http://hamptonroads.com/2008/09/massive-resistance-17-face-hostile-reception-schools-reopen.

Bird, David. "Queens Parents Conduct Classes at Closed School." *New York Times*, February 3, 1981.

"Boston Under the Phase I Plan." Watson.org, 1998, http://www.watson.org/~lisa/blackhistory/school-integration/boston/phase1.html.

Bremner, Robert Hamlett. *Children in America: A Documentary History, Volumes 1-3*. Cambridge, Mass.: Harvard University Press, 1974.

"Brown v. Board of Education." The National Center for Public Policy Research, http://www.nationalcenter.org/cc0725.htm.

"Busing and Strikes: Schools in Turmoil." *Time*, September 15, 1975, http://www.time.com/time/magazine/article/0,9171,917825-1,00.html.

"Busing's Boston Massacre." Hoover Institution, Stanford University, http://www.hoover.org/publications/policy-review/article/7768.

Caldas, Stephen J., and Carl L. Bankston. *Forced to Fail: The Paradox of School Desegregation*. Lanham, Md.: Rowman & Littlefield Education, 2007.

Canada, Geoffrey. "The Push-Back on Charter Schools." *New York Times*, March 14, 2010, http://roomfordebate.blogs.nytimes.com/2010/03/14/the-push-back-on-charter-schools/.

Carson, Clayborne. *Civil Rights Chronicle*. Lincolnwood, Ill.: Legacy Publishing, 2003.

"Charles C. Green et al. v. County School Board of New Kent County, Virginia." Encyclopedia Virginia, http://www.encyclopediavirginia.org/Green_Charles_C_et_al_v_County_School_Board_of_New_Kent_County_Virginia.

Chu, Daniel. "Changing Course." *Newsweek*, June 14, 1976.

Clotfelter, Charles T. *After Brown: The Rise and Retreat of School Desegregation.* Princeton, N.J.: Princeton University Press, 2004.

Collier-Thomas, Bettye. *Jesus, Jobs, and Justice: African American Women and Religion.* New York: Alfred A. Knopf, 2010.

Connelly, Matthew, and Paul Kennedy. "Must It Be the Rest Against the West?" Hudson, Florida, http://www.hudsonfla.com/west.htm.

Daniel Tatum, Beverly. *Can We Talk about Race? And Other Conversations in an Era of School Resegregation.* Boston: Beacon Press: 2007.

Davis, Seth. *When March Went Mad: The Game That Transformed Basketball.* New York: Macmillan, 2009.

Dawson, Sandra. "Desegregation without Despair." *Black Enterprise*, September 1978.

Editorial, *Jackson Daily News*, May 18, 1954.

"Education: More Trouble on The Busing Route." *Time*, September 1, 1975, http://www.time.com/time/magazine/article/0,9171,947171,00.html.

Feinberg, Lawrence. "Busing Orders Said To Widen Isolation." *Washington Post*, May 15, 1981.

Formisano, Ronald P. *Boston Against Busing: Race, Class, and Ethnicity in the 1960s and 1970s.* Chapel Hill: The University of North Carolina Press, 2004.

"14th Amendment." Cornell Law University, http://topics.law.cornell.edu/constitution/amendmentxiv.

"47-year-old Baton Rouge School Desegregation Case Finally Closes." *Jet*, September 8, 2003, http://findarticles.com/p/articles/mi_m1355/is_11_104/ai_107837336/.

Goldman, Peter. "The Roar of ROAR." *Newsweek*, June 9, 1975.

Hampton, Henry, and Steve Fayer. *Voices of Freedom: An Oral History of the Civil Rights Movement from the 1950s Through the 1980s.* New York: Bantam Books, 1990.

Heineman, Kenneth J. *God Is a Conservative: Religion, Politics, and Morality in Contemporary America.* New York: NYU Press, 1998.

Jackson, Kenneth T., Karen Markoe, and Arnie Markoe. *The Scribner Encyclopedia of American Lives.* Vol. 5, New York: Simon & Schuster, 2001.

Jan, Tracy. "Payzant Races to Finish." *Boston Globe*, November 1, 2005.

Johnson, Earvin "Magic," and Richard Levin. *Magic.* New York: Signet, 1991.

BIBLIOGRAPHY

Johnson, Kendra R. "African-American Richmond: Educational Segregation and Desegregation." Virginia Black History Archives, Virginia Commonwealth University, Special Collections and Archive-Cabell Library. http://www.library.vcu.edu/jbc/speccoll/vbha/school/turnage.html.

Kiviat, Barbara J. "The Social Side of Schooling." *Johns Hopkins Magazine*, April 2000, http://www.jhu.edu/jhumag/0400web/18.html.

Koff, Stephen. "Has Busing Outlived Its Usefulness?" *St. Petersburg Times*, January 31, 1991.

Maeroff, Gene I. "Boston's Decade of Desegregation Leaves Experts Disputing Effects." *New York Times*, December 28, 1984.

Masur, Louis P. "The Photograph That Shocked America, and the Victim Who Stepped Outside the Frame." March 2008, http://digitaljournalist.org/issue0803/the-photograph-that-shocked-america-and-the-victim-who-stepped-outside-the-frame.html.

Mathews, Jay. "Los Angeles Ends Forced Busing." *Washington Post*, April 20, 1981.

McCluskey, Neal P. *Feds in the Classroom: How Big Government Corrupts, Cripples, and Compromises American Education*. Lanham, Md.: Rowman & Littlefield, 2007.

McDonnell, Janet. *America in the 20th Century: 1970-1979*. Vol. 8, Tarrytown, N.Y.: Marshall Cavendish, 2003.

"Milliken v. Bradley." Cornell University Law School, http://www.law.cornell.edu/supct/html/historics/USSC_CR_0418_0717_ZD.html.

"Milliken v. Bradley." Courtroom View Network, http://lawschool.courtroomview.com/acf_cases/9667-milliken-v-bradley.

O'Connor, Thomas H. *South Boston: My Home Town*. Boston: Northeastern University Press, 1994.

Orfield, Gary, and Susan E. Eaton. *Dismantling Desegregation*. New York: The New Press, 1996.

Orfield, Gary. "Reviving the Goal of an Integrated Society." The Civil Rights Project, January 2009.

Pauley, Garth E. *The Modern Presidency & Civil Rights: Rhetoric on Race from Roosevelt to Nixon*. College Station: Texas A&M University Press, 2001.

Paulson, Amanda. "Resegregation of U.S. Schools Deepening." *Christian Science Monitor*, January 25, 2008, http://www.csmonitor.com/USA/Society/2008/0125/p01s01-ussc.html.

Peterson, Bill. "Issue of Busing Losing Its Sting Across Country." *Washington Post*, September 4, 1977.

Pride, Richard A. *The Burden of Busing: The Politics of Desegregation in Nashville, Tennessee*. Knoxville: University of Tennessee Press, 1995.

Reef, Catherine. *Education and Learning in America*. New York: Infobase Publishing, 2009.

Rossell, Christine H. *The Carrot or the Stick*. Philadelphia: Temple University Press, 1990.

Schemann, Serge. "White View of Queens School Clash . . . ." *New York Times*, February 17, 1981.

"School Busing." The Civil Rights Movement in Virginia, Virginia Historical Society, http://www.vahistorical.org/civilrights/busing.htm.

"Should School Busing Be Stopped?" *U.S. News & World Report*, September 30, 1974.

"'Statute of Limitations' for School Busing?" *U.S. News & World Report*, June 28, 1976.

Strouse, Jean. "Mean Streets of Boston." *Newsweek*, September 22, 1975.

———. *Newsweek*, May 5, 1975.

"Swann v. Charlotte-Mecklenburg Board of Education." Cornell University Law School, http://www.law.cornell.edu/supct/html/historics/USSC_CR_0402_0001_ZS.html.

Thernstrom, Stephan, and Abigail Thernstrom. *America in Black and White: One Nation Indivisible*. New York: Simon & Schuster, 1999.

Tyson, James L. "Chicago Considers Applying Brakes To School Busing." *Christian Science Monitor*, October 19, 1995.

Uhrich, Kevin. "Leaving No Child Behind." *Pasadena Weekly,* April 5, 2007, http://www.pasadenaweekly.com/cms/story/detail/?IssueNum=66&id=4509.

Werner, Leslie Maitland. "U.S. Says Cities Can Put an End to Busing Plans." *New York Times*, December 7, 1984.

Whitman, David. "Busing's Unheralded Legacy." *U.S. News & World Report*, April 13, 1992.

Wicker, Tom. "Busing After a Decade." *New York Times*, June 26, 1981.

Winningham, Geoff. "Football, Game of Life." *Texas Monthly*, October 1983.

Wisnia, Saul. *Fenway Park: The Centennial*. New York: St. Martin's Press, 2011.

Wohlsen, Marcus. "The First Day of Busing Was Lonely Day in Class." *Courier-Journal* (Louisville), September 4, 2005, courier-journal.com, http://www.courier-journal.com/article/20050904/NEWS01/509040418/The-first-day-of-busing-was-lonely-day-in-class.

Young, Rowland L. "Supreme Court Report: Supreme Court Ends Term on July 2 With a Flurry." *ABA Journal 68* (September 1982): 1150.

WEB SITES

http://www.nytimes.com/indexes/2004/01/18/edlife/index.html

This *New York Times* site features several articles relating to the 50th Anniversary of *Brown v. Board of Education*. Titles include "The Supreme Struggle," "Poetic Justice," "The Reluctant Icons," "Brown's Children's Children," and "When Busing Ends."

http://www.npr.org/templates/story/story.php?storyId=1853532

A three-part radio broadcast on "The Legacy of School Busing."

http://glencoe.com/sec/socialstudies/btt/brown/index.html

McGraw-Hill provides an interactive environment on this site where visitors can explore a variety of media including video, photographs, historical background, and other Web sites related to the Fiftieth Anniversary of *Brown v. Board of Education*.

http://www.adl.org/education/brown_2004

In a six-part lesson plan titled "Exploring the Promise of *Brown v. Board of Education* in Contemporary Times," the Anti-Defamation League challenges high school students to investigate whether segregation is a problem that we once lived with or still live with in U.S. schools.

http://www.pbs.org/wgbh/amex/eyesontheprize/story/21_boston.html

PBS's American Experience features "School Desegregation in Boston" on this site.

INDEX

PHOTO CREDITS

Cover: AP Photo
4-5: AP Photo
8: AP Photo
11: Courtesy of Library of Congress
14-15: AP Photo/J. Walter Green
18: Courtesy of Library of Congress
21: AP Photo
22: Courtesy of Library of Congress
26-27: AP Photo/Gene Herrick
30: AP Photo/Jack Thornell
32: Courtesy of Library of Congress
37: AP Photo/LK
38-39: AP Photo
41: AP Photo/Richmond Times-Dispatch, Bob Brown, File
45: Courtesy of Library of Congress
48-49: AP Photo
52: AP Photo
56: AP Photo/Frank C. Curtin
58: AP Photo
60: AP Photo/Peter Bregg
62: AP Photo
66: Courtesy of Library of Congress
69: AP Photo/Henry Griffin
71: Courtesy of Library of Congress
74-75: AP Photo
78: AP Photo/Frank Curtin
80: Courtesy of Rafael Amado Deras
82: AP Photo
84: AP Photo/Edward Kitch
89: AP Photo
91: AP Photo/Ted Powers
93: AP Photo
98-99: AP Photo/Tom Gannam
102: AP Photo/Mel Evans
106: AP Photo/Julia Malakie
110-111: Courtesy of Jim Henderson

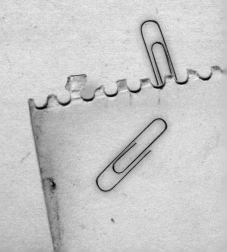